RAISING THE HANDICAPPED CHILD

Laura Pearlman and Kathleen Anton Scott

Prentice-Hall, Inc., Englewood Cliffs, New Jersey 07632

To Mark and Jerry,
For their constant inspiration, support, and love.

We would like to thank all the families who have contributed so much to our professional and personal growth by sharing their experiences with us. It is their courage and honesty that have made this book possible. We are very grateful for the privilege of knowing them.

    For the challenging and joyous personal experience of parenting, love and thanks to Belinda, Marc, and Brent.

Raising the Handicapped Child
by Laura Pearlman and Kathleen Anton Scott
Copyright © 1981 by Laura Pearlman
and Kathleen Anton Scott

Address inquiries to Prentice-Hall, Inc.,
Englewood Cliffs, N.J. 07632
Printed in the United States of America
Prentice-Hall International, Inc., London
Prentice-Hall of Australia, Pty. Ltd., Sydney
Prentice-Hall of Canada, Ltd., Toronto
Prentice-Hall of India Private Ltd., New Delhi
Prentice-Hall of Japan, Inc., Tokyo
Prentice-Hall of Southeast Asia Pte. Ltd., Singapore
Whitehall Books Limited, Wellington, New Zealand
10 9 8 7 6 5 4 3 2 1

Library of Congress Cataloging in Publication Data
Pearlman, Laura.
  Raising the handicapped child.
  Includes index.
  1. Handicapped children. 2. Children—Management.
3. Handicapped children—Family relationships.
I. Scott, Kathleen Anton. II. Title.
HQ773.6.P4   649'.151   81-4452

ISBN 0-13-752717-9 AACR2

Introduction

Our work has provided us with a unique opportunity over the past few years. It is unusual for medical or educational professionals to have the kind of involvement that we have experienced with the families of our patients.

We presently function as part of a team of professionals which includes several educators, a social worker, psychologist, occupational therapist, physical therapist, and speech pathologist. We work with children with all types of handicapping conditions; some of our patients are as young as three weeks old.

Our patients are not brought to a sterile office or clinic to wait their turn among many, separated by closed doors and shutters from the "sacred" people in white. We go to their homes. We are on their territory, where they feel unintimidated, safe, and comfortable. We wear our blue jeans, for in the course of our treatment we may be crawling on floors or changing a diaper. Brothers and sisters may be joining in our activities, the phone may ring, or visitors may drop in. This is where parents, siblings, relatives, and friends need to make the adjustment to living with and caring for a handicapped child. It is here in his home that we teach.

Our book is written for all those who share the common concerns that are addressed in its pages, concerns that are voiced over and over again by every family we visit.

We have included factual information which we, as pediatric specialists, need to be aware of so that we can act as a resource to families regarding children's rights and opportunities. We decided against listing agencies and organizations because we felt that it would be far too limiting. What we attempted to do, however, is describe what should be available in the way of education, vocational training (jobs), financial aid, medical treatment, and social organizations. Throughout the country laws and programs for handicapped citizens are changing and changing rapidly. We hope that by telling you what to look for, you will be able to do your own legwork. All else that is written is based on the sharing of information that took place in the homes of our patients and in meetings with professional team members, where countless hours are spent discussing the issues involved in raising a handicapped child.

We trust that as you read our book, you will recognize that many of the parents and professionals we work with have an honest feeling of hope for handicapped children and adults. This apparently stems from the fact that the architectural and social barriers are being broken down. It is time to continue to raise the consciousness of our society. To do so you, as a parent, will need the information that will help you prepare your child in the best possible way for a society that will recognize his potential, that will provide him with equal rights, equal protection under the law, and equal opportunities for education and employment—a society that is now preparing to accept him when he is ready to enter the adult world. This is the basis for the feeling of hope so many of our parents have expressed to us.

Our book is basically a book of sharing. Our families have gained emotional support by sharing their experiences, feelings, and ideas with each other. They have become more confident and assertive because we have shared our professional knowledge. By sharing our knowledge and their experiences with you, it is our hope that you too will gain support and confidence.

As we bring together our knowledge and the ideas of the parents we have worked with, we are confident that we will also be sharing some of the hope, inspiration, and remarkable courage that is inherent in meeting the challenge of raising a handicapped child.

Laura Pearlman
Kathleen Anton Scott

Contents

1. COPING

From the moment the pregnancy is confirmed, you begin to identify yourself as a parent. You review all of your preconceived notions of what it means to be a mother or father. As the pregnancy advances, an awareness develops that this child-to-be is indeed a different and separate individual. In time, you may even begin to attribute various characteristics and qualities to your anticipated infant. You begin to plan the nursery, arrange for diaper service, even select a name.

These feelings create a welcomed anticipation for your newborn. You will probably experience them whether this is your first child, second child, or tenth child. You are preparing yourself for your role as a mother or father. At times you may become frightened or nervous regarding the task you have taken on. It is likely, however, that overall your feelings will remain positive, your confidence will remain unshaken. If you are the mother, even into the final months, when you feel as though you will never regain your shape and you are always aware of the bulge in front of you, your eager anticipation of the arrival of your baby compensates for any discomfort or unpleasant feelings you have.

Labor is the sign that the time has come. You and your spouse have your list of phone calls to be made. Soon all those who love you and who share in your happiness and your lives will know that the child you have waited for is born.

Whether it is in the hospital, soon after delivery, or some months later, finding out that your child is not normal is a bitterly

— painful and shocking experience. The news may be told to you by a sympathetic doctor who answers your questions and offers some emotional support during the first devastating moments. It may be told to you by a doctor much more abrupt and short in his manner, presenting it to you in a matter-of-fact way. Regardless of how you find out, you are probably unprepared for the impact of the news, and perhaps it is difficult for you to accept.

The problem may be given a name. It may be an "impairment"—speech, visual, or hearing. It may be a problem noted at birth, such as Down's syndrome or cerebral palsy. Sometimes the problem remains nameless and is merely called a "delay." It may be a more subtle problem noted in later months or years, such as a learning disability. Possibly it is a combination of several problems— a multiple handicap. Often no explanation can be found in the medical history.

What is the reaction to such news? Most often the initial reaction, along with shock, is denial: "I can't believe it." "This can't be happening." With shock and denial come many questions: "Why did this happen?" "Will it go away?" "Can it be cured?" "What will we do?" And, along with shock, denial, and questions, come tears— tears of parents who must face the fact that the hopes, the expectations, and the dreams they had for their child will not become realities; tears that drown out the fantasies of watching your Little League player get his first base hit or your little ballerina at her first recital; real and seemingly endless tears. Those first tears do end. But there are many more to follow—more tears of frustration and hopelessness, and also tears of joy.

Now the unthinkable has happened and you are probably unprepared. Your feelings are so different from what you have experienced before that they may frighten you. You will wonder whether your feelings are the same kinds of feelings that other parents in your position have felt.

From our experience, let us look at an example of what commonly occurs.

Sue, a young mother of an eighteen-month-old child, realized that her baby was not responding to her in the same way her other children had. The baby would not turn her head as Sue shook a rattle or spoke in soft tones. The baby was tested and diagnosed as having a hearing impairment. Sue refused to believe the diagnosis. She stated that "the test was wrong." She thought the baby was too young to be tested. Despite reassurance by her doctor that the test was valid, despite encouragement by her husband, Sue refused to allow further testing. Several months went by and Sue finally was persuaded to retest the infant's hearing. Soon after the child was fitted for an aid.

Was Sue being stubborn or foolish? Was she a "bad mother"? How could she not listen to doctors and her husband? Why didn't she let them retest the child sooner? Answers to these questions and questions like them vary from person to person. We do not think that Sue was being a bad mother. She was not ignoring her husband's suggestion because she thought him to be foolish. Rather, she needed some time to deal with her feelings. Her feelings were typical of many parents who have had similar experiences. In time, she was able to face the reality of the situation and request a second hearing test.

Accepting your feelings can be very difficult at times. You may wonder, "Did I cause my child's handicap because I really didn't want to be pregnant?" "Was I such a bad father or husband that I was given this child as a punishment?" "How could my body, my genes, produce something that was not perfect?" Parents of handicapped children commonly agonize over such questions and then are faced with dealing with the guilt they elicit.

There may be times when you feel depressed, feeling as though there is no way to cope with yourself and your family. You may feel that all the burden has fallen only on you. You may begin to doubt your skills as a parent.

It is common for parents to relate episodes such as the following:

I was having a particularly bad day. It was sunny and warm and I wanted to finish my housework so I could rest with a book outside. The baby was sleeping and I thought I could put off his feeding for a half hour longer. Just as I settled down out back, he woke up. There was no way to calm him, so I prepared his meal and began to feed him. It usually takes about a half hour or forty-five minutes. As I sat there feeding him I began to get upset. First I was mad at myself for not planning the day better. Then I became mad at my husband for not helping me more with the housework so my days wouldn't be so full with things to do. I kept trying to rush things and that only made things worse, as the baby started to cry. It scares me now that I think about it, but I was really mad at my baby, too. Mad because at his age he should be able to feed himself. I was angry that he was taking up so much of my time. I kept thinking, "Why me?"

This example tells us quite a bit. The mother was saying that she became frustrated and angry. Her feelings were directed toward herself, her husband, and finally her child.

Was it really this mother's fault that she had not planned her day well, or was this simply an unusual day? Was it really that her husband did not help enough, or was it that because of this day she was in need of more help? It is easy for this mother to see that the child himself was not at fault. Had this mother recognized her anger as a human reaction to the stresses of the day, she would have been better able to cope with the guilt this incident aroused about her attitude toward her husband and her child.

COPING WITH YOUR FEELINGS

Probably for as long as you ever thought about becoming a parent, even as a child playing house, you had fantasies about what it would be like to have your own child, how you would love and care for him, how you would discipline him, what you would share together and what kind of a parent you would be.

During pregnancy, while there is always a deep, hidden, unspoken fear that something may go wrong, we hardly acknowledge it; we plan ahead as though everything will be perfect.

All of us question our ability as parents. Will we be "good" parents? Even though we had our own parents as models, we feel uncertain. We want to do some things differently from the way our parents did them, and in some ways we want to be exactly the same as our parents.

The problem of fulfilling the parental role when you have a child with special needs is unique. You cannot relate to your own childhood experiences, nor can you identify with your preconceived ideas about parenting. It is no wonder you feel angry, frustrated, and frightened. You do not know what to do. You may feel unable to assume this parental role at all. As one mother expressed it to us, she did not feel she was "up to it."

The initial step in learning to cope is to accept in yourself whatever it is you are feeling. Feelings of guilt, fear, anger, depression, and frustration are all normal. It is important that you realize this and that you not berate yourself if you experience these feelings.

As time goes on and the initial shock wears off, do not expect these feelings to disappear. Each time you encounter a situation with your child in which you feel at a loss, not knowing how to handle things, these feelings may reappear. Accept them, understand them, and reassure yourself that they are normal. You are not a "bad" parent because you have them; you are simply human. As you read on, we hope you will discover some of the problems that cause such feelings.

Sometimes you may vent these feelings on others. You may argue with your spouse, holler at other children, or withdraw from people. It has been told to us by parents that resolving such conflicts as they happen, rather than allowing the situation to snowball, alleviates a great deal of tension. An open and honest approach seems to be the best one.

Go to whomever has been the object of your outburst or withdrawal. Tell them honestly that you were simply feeling bad at the time. You will be surprised at how understanding and sensitive others are of your feelings. Even young children appreciate your willingness to admit you are human.

Mrs. S. told us about this situation in her home.

My husband will not do anything with our handicapped child. I can't even feed Julie when he is in the room. He won't hold her or play with her. He won't even watch anything on TV about handicapped people. I cannot talk about Julie's problem with him; he gets too upset.

This was a difficult situation for all. Because the total responsibility for the care and nurturing of the child was left to the mother, she naturally became resentful toward her husband, and their relationship suffered. Had he openly and honestly expressed his feelings to his wife, she might have realized that the problem did not stem from his not loving his child, but rather from loving her so much. It was easier for him to remove himself than to face the sadness he felt about her being the way she was. If he had been able to communicate this, they could have been closer and more supportive of each other's feelings.

Recognizing and accepting your own needs is essential. You also need to recognize and accept the feelings of your spouse. The strain on your marriage will become evident in time. The birth of a child with a handicap is not something either of you bargained for or wanted to happen. Now that it has happened, you must learn to deal with it separately and together.

Just as your feelings of anger and depression are acceptable, so are your spouse's. He/she is not becoming a bad parent, but rather is seeking to develop new attitudes, just as you are. These feelings are often similar to yours. However, they may not be demonstrated in the same way as your feelings. They may vary in intensity, becoming stronger or milder than your own. You probably will not have the same feelings at the same time. In other words, you may not both be angry or both feel guilty simultaneously. Because of this, it may be difficult to understand what your spouse is feeling. Talk with each other and express your feelings. You are both good parents. You are both experiencing something new and frightening.

Being supportive of each other is essential. Beginning from the basis that you both love your child, learn to respect and accept those feelings which may not have been so strong in rearing your other children. With this basis, you can seek support in each other. You can learn to become more tolerant of each other's feelings.

DEVELOPING ATTITUDES

Once you are acceptant of your feelings and dealing with them openly, the next step in learning to cope is to start developing some new attitudes about people with handicaps. Before you can do this, however, you must examine your present attitudes. We suggest the following exercise to help you get in touch with attitudes you have unconsciously developed over the years. Do *not* read the entire exercise through! Complete each step in the order that it is listed without reading further.

Step 1. Take five pieces of paper and number them 1–5. Take page number one and write the phrase "Handicapped child" across the top in large letters. Now write down the first ten thoughts that come to your mind as you look at the phrase.

Step 2. Take page number two and write the phrase "Normal healthy child" across the top in large letters. Again, write down the first ten thoughts that come to your mind as you look at that phrase.

Step 3. Take your third piece of paper and write your child's name across the top in large letters. Finally, write down the first ten thoughts that come to your mind as you look at his or her name.

Step 4. Go back now to your first piece of paper with the phrase "Handicapped child" on it. Put a + next to each positive thought listed and a − next to each negative thought you listed. Take your second paper with the phrase "Normal healthy child" on it and the third paper with your child's name on it and do the same.

Step 5. Take your fourth piece of paper. Divide it in four columns. Head the first column "Handicapped—positive." Write all your thoughts from your first sheet of paper (Handicapped child) that have a + next to them in this column. Head the next column "Handicapped—negative." Write all thoughts from your first sheet of paper that have a − next to them in this column. Head the third column with your child's name—positive and the fourth column with your child's name—negative. Proceed as you did with your first and second columns, putting all thoughts from your third paper (your child's name) in the appropriate column, either positive or negative.

Step 6. Take page five and divide it into four columns. Head the columns as follows: 1) Normal healthy child—positive, 2) Normal healthy child—negative, 3) your child—positive, and 4) your child—negative. Record your thoughts as before in the appropriate column from your second and third pieces of paper.

At this stage of the exercise, you have written down and separated positive and negative thoughts that occurred to you spontaneously about children with handicaps, normal healthy children, and your own child. You have completed one half of the exercise on examining your present attitudes. To complete the second half, proceed as follows:

Step 7. Answer the following questions: 1) How many negative thoughts did you have regarding handicapped children? Normal healthy children? Your own child? 2) How many positive thoughts did you have regarding handicapped children? Normal healthy children? Your own child? 3) Are there any thoughts about your child that are the same or similar to those you had about handicapped children? If so, what were they? 4) Are there any thoughts about your child that are the same or similar to those you had about normal healthy children? If so, what were they?

You have now compared your positive and negative thoughts about "normal" and "handicapped" children to your own child. The goal of the exercise you have done is to examine your present attitudes about a child with a handicap, one without a handicap, and to determine how you see your own child in terms of each.

Based on what you have written, does your child appear to you at present to have more similarities to a child with a handicap or more similarities to a normal healthy child? In other words, are your attitudes about your child based predominantly on his having a handicap? Are you seeing your child as a total child, independent of his handicap?

What you have discovered about your present attitudes in doing this exercise can now help you in the process of developing new attitudes.

We strongly encourage you to view your child as a special child, but not as a handicapped child. Rather, view him as a child *who has a handicap.* View him as your child who is special. He is not a "cerebral palsied child" or a "Down's syndrome child," but rather a child who has cerebral palsy or a child who has Down's syndrome. If your child had a broken leg, you would not think of him as a "fractured child." You would say he had a fractured leg. Your child has special needs based on a particular problem. The problem is certainly a part of your child and you cannot ignore it. The problem, however, is by no means the essence of the total child. He exists as a person first and foremost.

To foster this attitude, we suggest that you not refer to your child as a cerebral palsied child or a Down's syndrome child, and that you discourage others from doing so. Instead, say your child has cerebral palsy, Down's syndrome, or whatever is appropriate in your particular case. Look at him first as a child independent of his handicap, then as a child who has a special need.

Most parents anticipate their child's future based on a set of goals they have determined. While we can make guesses as to the potential abilities of a child with a handicap, we make them cautiously. Try not to think in terms of "What will my child be able to do several years from now?" Look instead to this day, this month, this year. Taking each day as it comes and watching your child grow to fulfill his potential can be rewarding, much more so than agonizing over how much he won't accomplish in the future. Likewise, it tends to foster a healthy and accepting attitude for yourself, your spouse, and your children.

As you watch your child develop each day, you will probably notice that he uses all of his strengths and abilities in everything he does. While his day-to-day accomplishments may seem minimal and slow, he is putting forth his very best efforts. He may make fifty or more attempts at standing up, dressing himself, or writing his name. Most of us would get discouraged after five attempts at a new task. If we did not realize some degree of success, we would quit. Our experience with children who have handicaps is that they do not quit. They try again and again. Each day, in every task, the effort is apparent. How often have you heard it said about the average child, "If only Johnny would apply himself, he could do so much better." A child who has a handicap usually does apply himself. To progress, he *must* do so every inch of the way. You can feel proud that your child will most likely use more of his potential, whatever that may be, than most people.

ORGANIZING YOUR TIME

One of the most difficult issues to cope with in parenting the child with special needs is the many physical demands that are placed upon the parents. Often there are medical problems to which you must attend. Feeding may take an exceptionally long time, to the point that you feel you have barely finished one meal when it is already time for another. It may be necessary to prepare special foods. Many children have very poor sleeping patterns and may awaken you often during the night, robbing you of much-needed sleep. These kinds of physical demands in themselves are exhausting.

Most couples spend time fulfilling their parental role, doing household chores, and earning a living. The anticipation of a reward helps us to deal with the stresses that are inherent in carrying out our daily routine. In the case of a job, the reward is a paycheck. In the case of parenting, the reward is increased independence. When a child takes his first step or says his first word, our efforts seem repaid and worthwhile. In the case of the handicapped child, however, it is not always so. It often seems that there is not any reward. It seems that the endless hours of effort are fruitless. In the case of the severely handicapped, not only does independence seem to be an impossible dream, but often these children are not even able to acknowledge your love and affection. It is very difficult to give your effort and your love when the reward is not apparent. Day after day of such an existence would shake the strongest among us.

Finding a reasonable solution to the problem of meeting the demands placed on you and gaining some personal satisfaction is not easy. If you are a person who does not usually organize your time well, it will be necessary for you to change. While change is never easy, the result will be worth your effort. Arranging a schedule and sticking to it is the first necessary step. Naturally there must be some flexibility for special occasions.

When attempting to arrange a schedule you must include 1) time needed for household chores and earning a living, 2) time for necessary parental care of all your children, 3) time for you and your spouse to enjoy each other, and 4) time for you to do the things you enjoy doing alone. It may seem that you will need more hours than there are in the week to fit in all of these things. If you organize your time and work cooperatively, however, it can be done.

Regarding household chores, we have several recommendations. Chores can be shared by all able family members. Dividing them among yourselves will spread responsibilities evenly. This will avoid overburdening one family member. Alternating responsibilities among children helps to avoid arguments about who is doing the most housework. Husbands and wives can divide their chores based on what is most practical for each to do.

When chores necessitate leaving home, they are best done on an evening or weekend when both the husband and wife are around, so that one parent can remain at home with the children. Taking children along to do such things as grocery shopping is usually an annoying experience. Running outside errands is accomplished much more quickly and efficiently when the parent is not distracted.

Plan a schedule so that a weekly routine is established for doing cooking, cleaning, laundry, and shopping. For example, if you plan your weekly menu ahead of time, it will be simple to prepare a grocery list from it. With this grocery list your shopping can be limited to once a week. Cooking, too, can be handled systematically. You already have your menu for the week and your ingredients. Many meals that require much preparation time can be cooked in double portions and one portion refrigerated or frozen. Also, prepare more than enough for each meal so that on weekends there are leftovers for a smorgasbord.

You can see from the example about shopping and cooking that you can considerably reduce time spent on such chores by sharing, scheduling, and planning.

Other hints that will make household chores a little easier are the following: 1) When you purchase clothing, be sure you get fabrics that do not require ironing. 2) If you can, reduce the amount of dish washing by using cooking vessels such as Pyrex or Corning Ware in which you can cook, serve, and store. 3) Lower your housekeeping standards a little if you must. Keep things as neat, orderly, and dust free as you can, and two or three times a year do a thorough housecleaning while someone watches the children for you. With these suggestions in mind, you may devise many ways to reduce time spent doing household chores in your particular situation.

Next, let us look at time spent parenting. This will of course depend on such things as how many children you have, in what various activities they are involved, and their ages.

Children, whether they are of school age or preschool age, should be awakened at a specific time each day so they fit into your planned schedules.

All children need time each day when they are left on their own to entertain themselves. This includes your handicapped child. Place him someplace where he is safe and comfortable, and check on him occasionally. If you do not attend to constant unnecessary interruptions, your children will soon learn this time is for independent play. Do not think you must entertain your handicapped child constantly because he cannot play with toys or watch TV. Provide him, during this time, with some auditory (something he can hear) or visual (something he can see) stimulation or toys he is able to play with, and leave him on his own. Often handicapped children develop independence of some kind or another during this time when they are left totally to their own resources.

You should also set aside time for each child during the week that is your time together. This time is very important to each child. What is most important, however, is not the quantity but the quality of the time spent. Five minutes spent truly enjoying each other is far more beneficial than five hours when you feel pressured and tired. This time can be set aside for each child on a particular day when you can plan to play a game, read a book, bake a cake, or whatever the two of you enjoy doing.

Bedtime can be a very enjoyable time for the whole family. It can be a time when you all do something quiet together for a few minutes, when you have a ritual of "tucking in," and when the children are given special hugs and kisses.

Your handicapped child can be treated in all ways the same as other children with a few exceptions. If someone must feed him, it would be best at dinner time to feed him separately before the rest of the family. Then, whoever has fed him can relax and enjoy dinner. While the rest of the family is eating, he can remain in the room in his chair with something to occupy him so he is included in your time together at dinner. If it is difficult to confine him and he is causing a disturbance, do not feel uneasy about removing him from the room for that time. Again, during your dinner time try not to attend to unnecessary interruptions, although they may be difficult to ignore and annoying at first. Dinner can be an enjoyable family time together.

After dinner may be a good time to do any special therapy your child needs. This is something that each capable family member should be taught to do, and the responsibility should be shared. The therapists and teachers can teach one parent the exercises or activities that need to be done; he, in turn, can teach them to other family members, who can do them together or take turns. Doing such therapy should not be a chore, but rather a loving and giving experience.

In summary, time devoted to parenting can be very productive if, like other responsibilities, it is well planned. Plans can include time children spend alone, time you share with each child individually, time together as a family, and time spent caring for the special needs of a family member.

Raising a child with a handicap can infringe upon your time so much so that you may miss quiet times you once had alone with your spouse. Set a special time each day for you and your spouse to talk quietly and privately. This need only be a fifteen-minute phone call at a favorable time of the day. It may be early in the morning or late at night, but it is not time spent while you are watching TV or doing the dishes. It is your time alone and together without the children, without the housework. It is not a time to discuss problems, but rather to simply enjoy one another.

There may be times when you and your spouse want to go out with friends or by yourselves. For such occasions, you should establish a resource for qualified baby-sitters. They are available and should be found so you will feel comfortable about leaving your child. An ad in the local newspaper requiring references, followed by a personal interview for which you have prepared questions, will sometimes bring results. Local colleges, churches, or synagogues often know people who would be interested in both earning extra money and having an educational experience with a handicapped child—particularly colleges where nursing, physical therapy, occupational therapy, or child development is taught. Sometimes an arrangement can be made with another parent or couple who will exchange sitting services with you. Most local phone directories list baby-sitting agencies. If you obtain a sitter via this method, references and an interview should be required. Incidentally, these same resources can be used to obtain baby-sitting services when both parents work. Day-care services can also be investigated in the same manner.

Next, let us look at the time you need to spend alone. The amount of this time will vary from person to person. Some enjoy and need more time alone than others. Recognize the amount of time you need for yourself and schedule it accordingly.

If you work full time, you may find yourself using your lunch hour to fulfill part of this need. You may want to set aside an early morning coffee hour or a time later in the evening. If you have a hobby or interest, it may require a period of time on the weekend. Scheduling this time alone into your weekly routine will help you to relax and enjoy it.

If you are at home, you probably will have more flexibility within your routine. Use the times when your children are playing independently or napping. Take advantage of the flexibility of your schedule so that you have time to spend doing things you enjoy. Not everyone participates in a hobby or sport. Most people, however, do have an interest—it may be something you do alone at home, such as reading or watching a movie on TV, or it may be an outside interest such as collecting certain items or playing golf. Often as our schedules become full and time becomes scarce, we find ourselves eliminating such personal interests for "more important things." Eliminating your personal time, however, may frustrate you more than help you. Rather than cutting back on this time, consider the possibility of finding a sitter, or schedule your time alone so that your spouse can watch the children.

Become conscious of the amount of time you need to spend alone. Plan for it as you do for your other commitments. It is an important and necessary part of your schedule.

In this chapter we have suggested that you make some changes in your life-style. The changes involve your feelings, your attitudes, and the way in which you use your time. It may be hard for you to make these changes simply because change of any kind is difficult. But remember—you have already changed your life-style as a matter of necessity. You are already coping somehow. The point is to make positive change, to handle things in the most comfortable and effective way, to base your life on your strengths and not on your limitations.

The ideas we have shared are those that have helped other parents with handicapped children to find more contentment and happiness in their parental roles and their personal lives.

Finally, there is an element of coping that cannot be omitted. In every life there are times to be humorous, joyous, and even silly. Special parents have more right to enjoy such times than most. Do not deny yourself pleasure and fun. You well deserve it

2. SIBLINGS, RELATIVES, AND FRIENDS

Your personal adjustment is not an isolated experience. It is a process that takes place amid the people who share in your life: your spouse, your other children, your relatives, and your friends. In the first chapter we talked about making this adjustment within yourself. We discussed the feelings many of our parents shared with us and ways in which they began to cope on a day-to-day basis.

Parents have also shared with us experiences they have had with their children, families, and friends. Many felt that incidents such as jealousy between siblings, unwanted advice from relatives, and the daily struggles of budgeting their time would have taken place in their families as a matter of course.

Other parents, however, felt that there were unmistakable differences in raising a handicapped child. These differences centered around explaining that their child had a handicap, and how that handicap affected their lives.

Explaining a handicap to children, relatives, and friends was often difficult. It was difficult trying to tell a young child in terms he understood. It was difficult asking older children to cope with a fact that they as adults could not yet cope with. It was not easy to tell their families and friends, and more often than not it was even more awkward to deal with the reactions and responses from them, often pitiful and patronizing words.

In retrospect, most of our parents felt that it was they themselves who set the tone regarding their handicapped child,

15

realizing that in many cases feelings came through regardless of the actual words they were saying. Because of this, they tried to establish an open and honest communicative system within the family. They struggled to achieve a balance so that they were able to work and play as a family. They were watchful of setting a good example for others. They explained to us that by doing these things, they were able to convey a positive attitude about their child to their families and friends.

In this chapter we have combined the experiences most commonly shared with us into a sample case study to illustrate how others may be affected and what effect you can have on helping others cope.

Sharon is a two-and-a-half-year-old girl with curly brown hair that Mrs. P. combs into pigtails and ties with bows to match her outfit. Her eyelashes curl upward over big brown eyes. Wherever she goes with Mr. and Mrs. P., people cannot help but remark about what a beautiful child she is. Sharon has a diagnosis of mixed athetoid and spastic cerebral palsy. She is unable to move her arms or legs for any purposeful movement. She cannot feed herself, and when fed has difficulty swallowing.

Sharon's brothers, David and Aaron, are now eight and ten years old. One afternoon Aaron came home from school and told Mrs. P. he had made a new friend. He asked if he could invite his new friend for dinner the following day. Mrs. P. happily responded, "Sure." Satisfied, Aaron went outside. A few minutes later he returned, and approaching Mrs. P., said, "But Mom, what about Sharon?"

Mrs. P. knowing what Aaron's question meant, was caught off guard. Aaron had invited friends over many times and had never before said anything about Sharon. She also knew that she and Aaron had talked many times in the last two years about Sharon having a handicap. After all, Aaron was seven when Sharon was born. Mrs. P. needed to explain many things and answer many questions about why Sharon did not walk and talk. Now things were different. This was not a neighborhood boy who knew the P. family and had been in and out of their home regularly to play. This boy had never been to their home. A situation had come up where Aaron obviously felt he would need to do some explaining and answer some questions— questions which made him feel uncomfortable.

Mrs. P. understood how Aaron felt. She had felt the same herself many times when for one reason or another a stranger came to her home and although no questions were asked, she felt compelled to say, "The reason my daughter is not walking around is because she has cerebral palsy."

She looked at Aaron lovingly and responded in a way that allowed him to express whatever it was that he felt inside. She asked him his own question, "What about Sharon?" "Well," Aaron said, "she's not like other kids." "No, she's not," said Mrs. P., agreeing with him and then remaining silent as he continued. "Well, she can't walk or talk," said Aaron. "Well, you know, Ma, she's got cerebral palsy." "You're right," said Mrs. P. again, waiting for Aaron to go on. "Well," said Aaron, pausing, "well anyway, she's my little sister and if John wants to be my friend he'll have to understand."

Mrs. P. hugged Aaron and he ran out the door, back to his play.

When Mrs. P. shared this story with us, it was obvious that she felt she had given Aaron the best reply. She had allowed him to answer his own question, to discover for himself the way he felt most comfortable in handling this situation. She appeared happy with his solution.

At ten, Aaron was aware of his sister's problem. What he was becoming increasingly aware of was how it affected him.

How does having a brother or sister who is handicapped affect a child? There are as many answers to that question as there are differences in children. Much will depend on the age of the child, his place in the family (oldest, middle, etc.), and his individual personality. Much will depend on how he sees his parents reacting to the handicapping condition.

In the chapter on coping, we touched on several points that involved the family. We mentioned that each child needs time alone with a parent, that it is important to share responsibilities between family members and to spend time together as a family. Doing such things on a routine basis creates an overall positive atmosphere in which children can learn and grow. The example of Aaron points out that while the overall family atmosphere may be very positive, problems and questions still arise. While you cannot be prepared for every question and problem, there are certain things you can do to create open and honest communication between yourself and your children so that problems can be aired and questions can be answered.

Let us look at a condensed history of what had taken place in the P.'s home prior to the incident described, when Aaron expressed concern about inviting his friend for dinner.

When Mrs. P.—Lynn—went to the hospital to give birth to Sharon, she assured David and Aaron that she would return in a few days with their new baby sister or brother. When Sharon was born and she did not breathe immediately, she was placed in the high-risk nursery. Naturally, the P.'s became concerned.

When Mr. P.—Don—called David and Aaron to tell them they had a new baby sister, Grandma answered the phone and immediately sensed that something was wrong. Don told her what was going on and then asked to talk to David and Aaron, who were then ages five and seven. On the phone he simply told them, in as happy a voice as he could muster, that they had a new baby sister.

"When will Mommy bring her home?" they asked. "Soon," said Don. When Don came home from the hospital that night he brought presents for David and Aaron from their new sister, read them a story and put them to bed. The next few days, while Lynn remained hospitalized, Don came home each night, did something special with David and Aaron, and answered their many questions about their new sister. "What does she look like? How big is she?"

In the meantime, the P.'s became increasingly worried. The pediatrician who initially examined Sharon had suspected problems. Within a few days he confirmed the P.'s fears. Sharon did not appear to be normal and she was medically very unstable.

During those first few days the phone at home rang often. Relatives and friends were calling—first to hear the good news, and later, when they found out about Sharon's problems, to ask how she was doing. Grandma and Don were careful to speak in low tones on the phone so David and Aaron could not hear what was being discussed. The night before Lynn was to come home from the hospital, Don read David and Aaron a story and then, becoming very serious, said he had to tell them something. They appeared to sense that what he was about to say was important, and they immediately quieted down, sitting close to him and looking directly at him.

"Mommy is coming home tomorrow," he began. As if they knew something more was to follow, David and Aaron did not become excited, but remained silent as he continued. "Sharon cannot come with her right now. She is sick and has to stay in the hospital until she is better."

The first difficult questions began. "What's wrong, Daddy? Is she going to die?"

"Well," responded Mr. P., "some babies are strong when they are born, and they are big enough to come home in a few days. Sharon is not very strong and she is very small. The doctors have to

help her get stronger and bigger before she can come home. Mommy and I will go to see her every day and tell you how she is doing. In the meantime, be good boys and go to bed now so you will be all ready to see Mommy tomorrow."

The boys kissed their father and obediently went to bed with no further questions.

In the weeks that followed Lynn's arrival home there were many phone calls and many quiet discussions. Lynn and Don visited Sharon daily, feeding and holding her as much as possible. Each night they reported to David and Aaron about how their sister was doing. "Today," they would say, "your sister drank almost all her milk. She is getting stronger every day. She is still not as strong as the other babies, but she is very cuddly and beautiful. If she could talk we know she would say, 'I want to see my brothers.'"

Each day the P.'s spent some special time with David and Aaron, time when they did not talk about Sharon, time when they talked about school and friends and read stories.

After two months of Don and Lynn's very difficult schedule between hospital and home, Sharon was discharged. Upon Sharon's arrival home, David and Aaron ran to greet her with cards they had made, with Grandma's help, which said, "Welcome home, Sharon, we love you!" They stared as Lynn removed Sharon's blanket, examining her carefully and appearing amazed at how tiny she was (she weighed only six pounds at two months old). Don and Lynn sat them both down on the couch, positioned their arms and allowed each of them to hold her for a few moments.

For the next few days, after school David and Aaron followed Lynn around, watching and occasionally touching a hand or foot as Sharon was fed, bathed, changed, and rocked. They took turns holding her several times a day. At night they continued to have special time alone with their parents.

After a few days of this routine, life for David and Aaron began to resume as before. They played outdoors after school, checking on Mom and Sharon every once in a while, holding Sharon when they felt like it, and bringing a friend in occasionally to show off their new baby.

Within weeks after Sharon was home a routine was somewhat established. Each feeding took well over an hour because she had a very weak suck. Her sleeping schedule was erratic and Don and Lynn got very little sleep. But David and Aaron were given breakfast and sent off each morning as usual. Grocery shopping, laundry, house-keeping, and meals all got done somehow between feedings, and the *nightly ritual of time alone with each boy continued. As far as David and Aaron were concerned, things at home were as usual, with the one addition of a baby sister.*

Although things were falling into place so far as reestablishing a household routine that included Sharon's care, all was not resolved.

In the months that followed it seemed to Lynn that David, who before had eaten like an average five-year-old, occasionally spilling something, was almost nightly spilling his milk at dinner time. Aaron, who has asthma, appeared to be getting more frequent attacks that required medical attention. The boys seemed to be getting into more scraps with each other than usual. Don and Lynn, fatigued because of the frequent disruptions of their sleep, felt jumpy and on edge. The noise when the boys had playmates over annoyed them. The sounds of toys and running feet were intolerable. They were hollering at the boys more frequently. Even the sound of Sharon's cry as she awoke for a feeding elicited an occasional, "Darn it—she's up again."

Grandma, helpful and supportive, had many suggestions. "Why don't you change the nipple on her bottle, the hole is too small." "Put a sweater on her, she's too cold." "The formula isn't right, that's why she's vomiting." Grandma had an apparently endless repertoire of helpful comments.

Lynn began to resent the occasional Saturday or evening work that Don's job had always required. She felt that the responsibility of Sharon was falling unfairly on her.

Overall, an aura of tension appeared which before had not existed. Amidst the busy routine and somewhat uneasy atmosphere were the phone calls and visits of relatives and friends—some apparently fulfilling their obligation to politely inquire or bring the new baby a gift, and some appearing sincerely interested in sharing in the experiences the P.'s were having that centered around the new addition to their family. Don and Lynn welcomed calls and visits from certain people. Others made them very uncomfortable.

There was Lynn's sister Mary, who did not respond much when Lynn complained, but was always ready to listen. When Mary called, she always asked, "Can you talk now?" If Lynn answered no, an acceptant and loving, "Talk to you later" followed. Mary always asked about Sharon, David, Aaron, and Don when she called. She also used Lynn as her sounding board when she had problems. They had always been very close and shared each other's problems.

Then there was Don's friend Pat. Pat had worked with Don, and visited often to see how Sharon was doing. His questions about her were always followed with a patronizing pat on the back and, "If you need anything or you want to talk, you know I'm here." When Don would ask Pat how he or his family was, Pat often responded with a simple, "Oh, they're fine." Sometimes he would relate a problem that had come up in his family, but always when he did so, made certain to assure Don that he should not concern himself about it. "Yesterday my boy fell off his bike. He needed three stitches in his head. It was nothing. He's okay now. Gee, Don, why am I even telling you about it? You have enough to worry about. My little everyday problems are nothing next to yours."

Joan, an old schoolmate of Lynn's, was a frequent caller and visitor. Having shared many experiences with Lynn as they were growing up, she of course wanted to be actively included in this new phase of Lynn's life. Over the months Joan developed a talent for being very resourceful. Somehow she began "bumping into" people who had friends with children who had problems just like Sharon's. It seemed that almost weekly she heard of a new doctor, clinic, or hospital that specialized in treating children like Sharon. If she did not hand deliver newspaper and magazine articles dealing with handi-capped people's issues, they arrived in the mail with a note, "Thought you'd be interested. Love, Joan." Joan also had a great deal of advice in response to Lynn's account of particular events that occurred. "Why didn't you tell the doctor you can't wait a week and you want to see him tomorrow?" Or, "Find out from the druggist exactly what's in that prescription!"

The initial visits of relatives and acquaintances with whom the P.'s had not been close were generally awkward. After the polite smiles and phrases like "Isn't she adorable," Lynn and Don almost felt responsible for taking care of the obviously ill-at-ease visitors who seemed at a loss for words in this situation. They typically found themselves turning the conversation around to something other than Sharon—something all felt comfortable discussing, usually other family members or mutual friends: "Have you seen so-and-so re-cently? How's she doing?"

When the excitement of the first few months subsided, and the adjustment process became a natural part of everyday living, with its ups and downs, David and Aaron became more aware of Sharon as another person in the family. Questions like "When will Sharon sit up?" "When will she walk?" and "When will she be able to play with us?" all came up during the first year. David and Aaron had not forgotten what they had been told the first time Don had explained to them that Sharon had a problem. They asked, "When will she be as big and strong as she's supposed to be?"

Each time a question was asked, either Lynn or Don responded immediately. "We don't know when Sharon will do certain things. Remember, she is not very strong. Most babies do sit up by this age, but Sharon cannot because her muscles aren't ready to do that yet." Often such brief answers were enough to satisfy curiosity and there were no further discussions. Sometimes, however, David or Aaron wanted to know more. "Why isn't Sharon strong?" "Will she ever be as strong as me and David?" When either boy indicated he wanted to know more, he was given as much information as he desired. Many times when longer explanations were needed, the words cerebral palsy and handicapped were used to describe Sharon's problem. When they were first used they were defined in terms understandable to each boy.

On one occasion Lynn felt Aaron really wanted to know more about Sharon's condition than she herself could explain. She went to the library and borrowed several children's books about handicaps, and together she and Aaron read and talked about them. David, while appearing satisfied with shorter answers to specific questions, was overheard asking Aaron several times after his discussions with Lynn, "What were you and Mom talking about?" Lynn realized that David did not always ask questions as freely as Aaron, even though he too was curious. She didn't wait for him to ask questions, but watched carefully for opportunities to share information with him.

When it came to playing with Sharon, Don and Lynn found many games in which she could participate. Playing house was one activity in which Sharon could easily join with David and Aaron in spite of her limitations. She could be the baby, as in fact she was in their own family. Lynn often used this game to insure some peace and quiet when Sharon was napping and she wanted to relax herself. "You're the daddy, you're the brother and I'm the mommy. We all have to be very quiet now because the baby is sleeping." When Sharon was up and the family was together, she was included whenever possible in activities they were doing. If they played cards, Sharon and Mommy or Daddy played as partners. One of them would hold her in their lap and when it was Sharon's turn, they would take her hand and move it to pick up or put down a card. When Sharon and her partner won, hands were clapped in excitement. When they lost, heads were shaken with a "Too bad." When weather permitted and Sharon's health was stable, family outings were *frequent. From the sidelines, in the child-size wheelchair that was purchased when she was two, Sharon watched her brothers in Little League.*

The most recent issue that has come up between the three children is Sharon's dependence. "It's not fair," said David when asked to pick up all the toys (including Sharon's) one day. "Just because she's handicapped she doesn't have to do any work around here!" "You sound angry," responded Lynn. "I don't blame you. I feel angry too sometimes. Then I remember that Sharon cannot do certain things because of her handicap."

This rather lengthy account of the P.'s experiences brings to light many issues involving siblings, relatives, and friends. We have purposefully selected the case of a multiple handicapped child to get across several points which would not have otherwise been possible to illustrate. For example, while many experiences would be similar in the case of a deaf or blind child, the implications of such problems may be easier for young children to understand. Knowing that a brother or sister cannot see or hear has a somewhat built-in explanation of what to expect and what not to expect.

In the example we have chosen of the P.'s, there are many points we would like to discuss. It was probably obvious to you as you read that many things that happened in the family are typical of what happens In any family with the arrival of a new baby.

David's beginning to spill his milk so frequently, Aaron's asthma worsening, and the boys, arguing more when Sharon came home are typical examples of how the behavior of siblings may change upon the arrival of any new baby. Realizing that the baby is getting so much attention from everyone, particularly parents, children may begin to feel some insecurity about their place in the family. They may resort to negative behavior, acquiring ailments, developing new fears, or squabbling to gain the attention they fear they are losing or that they now have to share with another child. Such behavior may continue until they feel totally reassured of receiving equal love and attention. Older children may react to a lesser degree if they feel more secure about their position in the family.

Spending time alone with each child has been mentioned before. It is worthwhile mentioning it again, as it can help to reassure siblings that you do indeed continue to be aware of their needs and enjoy their company. This time may decrease the need for them to seek attention through negative behavior.

The "helpful" grandma is also typical of what goes on in many families. Grandparents often feel they are more experienced and capable than their children. Also, parents seem to always remain parents, almost compelled by some unknown force to continue giving "helpful suggestions" to their children. Even though you already have your own children, your parents may feel they know best. Perhaps sometimes they do. Surely the positive force that grandparents have on a child's life greatly outweighs any small annoyance they may be to you when they impose their suggestions on you.

The experiences we have just recounted are indeed typical of many families when a baby is born. Some experiences, however, are unique to a family that has a child with a handicapping condition.

What is unique about the P. case is the need to explain to people the difference between Sharon and the "normal" baby they had all expected, and then to deal with their responses.

Children, no matter how young, are extremely sensitive to their parent's emotional tone. During the time immediately following Sharon's birth, it is reported that David and Aaron behaved exceptionally well while their grandmother cared for them. When Don came home from the hospital each night they remained in close physical contact with him and were quiet. They were not as boisterous or active as usual. They appeared to sense that he was worried even before they were told about Sharon's problem. Closed doors and quiet conversations arouse curiosity in children, and when Don did tell them that Sharon was having problems, it was almost as though they were prepared for the news.

Explaining to your children exactly what is different about a brother or sister with a handicap is extremely difficult for several reasons. Finding terms that are understandable to them is problematical. Asking your children to accept an unpleasant reality of life, one for which you have no explanation, is in many cases stressful. Most parents, however, believe it is best from the start to explain to each child as much as he is capable of understanding.

In the case of the P.'s, Don used words like *strong* and *big*, words a five- or seven-year-old can comprehend. He told them as much as they needed to know, but did not go into long explanations. When subsequent questions came up, they were answered briefly, simply, and honestly. When Aaron made it known that he was ready to handle more information, Lynn found a way—through children's books—to give it to him. Some of the following examples may help you to find the right words.

Mrs. S. explained a physical handicap to three-year-old John:

It was dinner time, and John and his sister Mary were both at the table. Mrs. S. said, "John, I have to tell you something important. You know that you and Mary are different, right? Can you tell me some ways you are not the same? ... There is another way Mary is not the same as you. Can you see that Mary cannot move her arms and legs the same way you do? Mary may never be able to move her arms and legs like other children. You are each very special; we love you both very much."

Mrs. M. explained a mental handicap to five-year-old Suzie:

Mrs. M. was alone with Suzie after reading her a story. "Can we have a little talk now? Do you know how children learn to talk and count and then they go to school and learn to read and write? Well, I have something to tell you about your brother Tony. Tony cannot learn like that. Tony is different. He cannot learn things like most other children. Will you remember that? You and Tony both make me very happy; we love you both very much."

Mrs. L. explained blindness to three-year-old Tommy:

Mrs. L. was alone with Tommy after his bath. "Tommy, will you sit very quietly with me for a minute? I have something to tell you. You can show me your eyes. You see with your eyes. Do you know that your brother's eyes are different from your eyes? They are. He cannot see with them. If you close your eyes you cannot see. Terry can never see, even when his eyes are open. His ears are just like yours. He can hear with his ears. He just cannot see with his eyes. He is a good big brother and you are a good little brother. You're both such good boys."

The question "Why?" coming from a young child after a brief explanation can simply be answered, "That is just the way _____ was born. I don't know why."

Children who do not ask further questions after a brief explanation may have either heard what was said and accept that much for the time being, or perhaps they did not completely understand or hear what was said. In any case it seems important that something be said before children find out from someone other than their parents. Overhearing conversations in your home or hearing a remark made innocently by a neighbor could lead even a very young child to believe you have not been honest with him.

Older children can, of course, be given longer and more detailed explanations. The term *handicap* can be used, and the actual diagnosis can be told to older children. Again, there are children's books about some handicapping conditions that can be obtained through your library. Key words in explaining such a condition to your children are *different* and *cannot*. Such words imply that the limitations are not due to anything anyone did or did not do. Words to be avoided are *better* and *worse*, since such words imply that you are comparing your children. The word *won't* should also be avoided, as a small child might infer that his handicapped brother or sister really can do something but simply will not do it for some reason.

The point that has been emphasized by most parents is this: Do not put off telling your other children about the handicap until they ask. Tell them as soon as possible at an appropriate moment and provide additional information as you feel it is needed. It is up to you to establish the basis for open communication with your children.

How much you share and how comfortable you are with relatives and friends will depend to a great extent on the kind of relationship you already have established with them. Lynn and her sister Mary had obviously always been intimate and very honest with each other. Sharon's handicap did not change this. Lynn felt totally accepted by Mary. She was an attentive and interested listener, allowing Lynn to get all her feelings out into the open without judgment. What is important is that Mary continued to share her own life—both the good and the bad—with Lynn as before. She did not express sorrow or remorse. She did not assume that Lynn was wallowing in self-pity. She assumed that Lynn was the same caring, loving sister she had always been. Mary had confidence in Lynn's ability to handle her life with its ups and downs. Their relationship remained the same after Sharon was born.

Pat and Don had never been very close. Although sincerely concerned and well meaning, Pat's attitude and comments implied that Don must be so overwhelmed with his own problems that he no longer cared about other people. This created an uncomfortable feeling between them. It was as though Pat always assumed that Don was sad or upset. Don felt uneasy joking with Pat or telling him the cute things Sharon was doing. They had not been close before Sharon's birth, and soon after, when Don realized he felt depressed when Pat was around, he saw no reason to continue the friendship.

Lynn's schoolmate Joan found yet another way to deal with Sharon's differences. She had always given Lynn advice about her makeup, her boyfriends, her marriage, and her children. They had known each other for so many years that Lynn had become accustomed to Joan's advice. During the course of their long friendship she had learned to automatically tune Joan in and out depending on whether she cared to listen or not. Sharon's birth seemed to provide an opportunity for Joan to become a real expert. When it came to advice about Sharon, however, Lynn was unusually sensitive. She trusted her relationship with Joan enough to finally tell her that if she wanted information or advice from her she would ask for it. They remained good friends.

Relatives and acquaintances with whom you have had a distant relationship are probably handled best in a distant but honest manner. If you know they feel uncomfortable or awkward because of your child's handicap, you may want to ease this feeling by describing the handicap and answering their questions. An open approach on your part will encourage acceptance and understanding on their part.

Other awkward situations may arise, such as bumping into an old acquaintance or neighbor who does not know anything about your child. It is not necessary in such situations to make explanations unless a question arises that requires an explanation. For example, if your child is four years old and not walking or talking, someone may ask how old he is. "He's four years old now. He has a handicap. He's very special to us," is an honest and sufficient response.

Regardless of what your relationship is with relatives and friends, you need not allow yourself or your child to be treated in any way that is uncomfortable for you. If you feel your child is unreasonably spoiled or pampered by someone, you can discourage such treatment. If you feel someone pays particular attention to your handicapped child to the exclusion of your other children, you can let them know it disturbs you. If a certain person depresses you, you can openly discuss your feelings with him or avoid talking to him. You can control the balance and atmosphere in your home and your life by being honest with people.

What is also unique about the birth of a handicapped child is the emotional atmosphere that surrounds it. At first emotions may be more intense. For some, the intensity lessens as time goes on.

In the chapter on coping we mentioned that you may have feelings of anger, depression, guilt, and frustration. We also talked about you and your spouse being understanding and tolerant of each other's feelings. We are now going to talk about your children's feelings.

Depending on the ages of your children, they may experience all or many of the same feelings as you and your spouse. It is important for them that both of you be as understanding and tolerant of their feelings as you are of each other's. When David said angrily, "Just because she's handicapped, she doesn't have to do any work around here," Lynn realized that she too had felt angry many times when feedings took too long or her rest was interrupted. She related to David that she understood how he felt. She followed with a simple statement about how she handled her own anger: "Then I remember Sharon cannot do certain things." She recalled a simple fact. The message implied in Lynn's response to David is, "I accept your feelings. You are not a bad boy for having them." Such a response, void of judgment, opens the doors for the honest and open communication you want to establish. Had Lynn said, "That is a terrible thing to say; don't ever let me hear you talk like that again," it is likely that David would have kept his future feelings to himself. His anger would have been coupled with guilt, and he may have developed some resentment toward his sister. Instead he was made to feel accepted and human. His understanding and love for his sister were reinforced.

In dealing with relatives and friends you are probably aware of the different emotions they arouse in you. We have intimated that at times Lynn felt annoyed by her mother, comfortable with Mary, and angered by Joan. Don felt saddened by Pat. They both felt awkward with certain people. To deal with these emotions Lynn and Don needed to first recognize that other people were still adjusting to Sharon's handicapping condition.

Going back again to the chapter on coping, you recall how you separated your child's handicapping condition from his total being. The messages you convey to your children as well as to others are not only contained in the words you speak. Your tone of voice, the look on your face, and your body gestures say a great deal about the feelings behind your words. If you sound depressed every time you talk about your child to your spouse, your other children, or your relatives and friends, it is likely that you will convey the message that your child is a source of depression. If, however, you are able to talk joyously about your total child apart from the limitations of his handicapping condition, children, relatives, and friends will soon realize he is a source of joy and pride to you.

SUMMARY

In this chapter we have used the example of one family to illustrate the most common issues that parents have discussed with us concerning siblings, relatives, and friends.

Your attitude, your example, and your honesty appear to be the prevailing factors that will determine how your child is accepted by others.

Remember your initial fears and reservations based on mistaken and unfounded notions about handicapped people. Give your children, relatives, and friends an opportunity to learn as you did. Through honest sharing and your example, others will learn the truth about your child. They will become aware of his actual limitations and his special needs. They will become comfortable with their ability and yours to deal with these limitations and needs. They also will come to see your child apart from his handicap as the worthwhile, unique, and lovable person that he indeed is.

3. IDENTIFYING MEDICAL PROBLEMS

What is wrong?
Why did it go wrong?
What can we do?
Will it ever go away?
What will my child be like?

The questions seem so simple! If only the answers were as simple, perhaps the anxiety and fear associated with medical problems would ease. Medical decisions that you are likely to make will range from choosing a doctor to deciding upon a course of treatment (therapy versus medication; medication versus surgery). Making such decisions will not be easy, but we hope that by sharing the suggestions made by parents you will find the confidence you need.

Certain problems are easily identified at an early age. These are problems where a group of symptoms are present, or where the medical history of the child or family indicates the probability of a specific problem existing. For example, children who have Down's syndrome have particular physical characteristics in common and are therefore usually diagnosed at birth or soon after. Spina bifida is another condition that can be identified at birth, as can other physical anomalies (differences) that are visible to the examiner and/or parent. In addition to infants who have differences such as those noted, there are several other factors that may lead to the early diagnosis of a handicapping condition and/or medical problem. The history of a difficult pregnancy; the presence of disease or addiction during pregnancy; a difficult, unusual, or premature delivery; and a family history of a condition would be some of these factors. If any such factors are known to be present, the newborn infant is usually observed and examined carefully to determine if he is affected in any way.

Some infants have histories of such difficulties, but still do not exhibit immediate problems. Many physicians will then monitor the child's development, examining the infant periodically to make certain conditions and delays do not develop.

However, often problems are not obvious at an early age. They may be noted several months or even years later. They may not fit any particular picture or diagnosis. The pregnancy and delivery may be normal and there may be no unusual family history.

The signs and symptoms of a problem may at first be so subtle that you may wonder if you are not being overly concerned about what may simply be the child's unique personality.

Jenny was the fourth child born to the B.'s. She was a blond, six-pound-five-ounce baby delivered under local anesthetic following a normal pregnancy. Mrs. B. kiddingly remarked many times as the weeks passed following Jenny's birth that Jenny was "lazier" than her other babies had been. Because she was the youngest and everyone made such a fuss over her, it was felt that Jenny's "laziness" was simply the result of her not having to put forth much effort to get attention. Jenny rarely cried, and when she did her cry was rather soft. She drank her bottle very slowly since she did not even appear to put much effort into sucking. She did not pick up her head to look around, and at several months old still felt like a floppy infant, needing total body support when held or carried.

Although Mrs. B. joked about her "spoiled little princess," she began to feel uneasy about how different Jenny was than her other children had been at Jenny's age. At five months Jenny still was not lifting her head or rolling over, and Mrs. B. began to question her pediatrician. Her questions led to more careful examination, referrals to specialists, extensive testing, and many months of the agonizing waiting game—waiting for appointments, waiting for results, waiting for Jenny to miraculously begin moving about—waiting and wondering. Finally a diagnosis was made.

A brain scan revealed that Jenny was in fact brain damaged. The reason for her brain damage could not be traced to any particular cause or incident.

The case of Jenny is one in which there were no identifiable signs or symptoms at birth. Subtle signs noted a few months later, such as weak suck, weak cry, and inactivity, led to eventual testing which revealed a physiological abnormality.

Signs noted later in life such as poor response to sound or visual stimulation may lead parents to pursue testing that may result in a diagnosis of visual or hearing impairment. Similarly, children who are observed by parents to develop what appear to be spasms are often diagnosed through the use of the EEG test to have seizure disorders.

Justin S. had always been a busy child. At the age of four, his small frame darted about the house in continuous motion. It seemed, his mother said, that while everything fascinated him, nothing held his attention. Occasionally Justin would stop suddenly and stare into space. Mrs. S. said that Justin rarely paused long enough to finish a puzzle or look at a book, and it was not until very late at night that his blue eyes closed.

Mr. and Mrs. S. listened patiently to the many comments from their friends and relatives. "He will grow out of it." "You do not discipline him enough." "His uncle was that way and now look at him." But as time for his kindergarten registration crept up, they decided to seek out a neurologist—just to make sure.

The visit to the neurologist disturbed them. He was friendly and asked questions patiently, but made no diagnosis. He ordered an EEG and referred them to a psychologist within the clinic.

The psychologist tested Justin, but made no immediate diagnosis. He told the S.'s that they were to return in two weeks for a meeting where they would sit down and discuss the results of the testing. The S.'s reluctantly agreed to wait.

At the meeting, the reports given were very technical and full of jargon, but a diagnosis was made. Based on the test results, Justin was diagnosed as having seizures, along with hyperactivity. The S.'s were then given a few alternative treatments for the problem and asked to decide about medication, therapy, and special classes.

There are still other children who appear to have problems that do not fit any picture, cannot be traced to a cause, and whose test results appear to be normal. These are the most difficult children to diagnose. Often, in fact, no diagnosis is made. These children are said to have *developmental delays* of unknown etiology (for causes unknown). It is very frustrating for the parents of these children to wonder exactly what is wrong with their child.

As Michael crawled about the house on his second birthday his father, Mr. B., looked over his paper to watch him carefully. Michael's blond hair and blue eyes peered over the coffee table. He pulled himself up by it and began to play a game of peekaboo with his father. When Mr. B. gave no indication that he wanted to play the game, Michael dropped back to the floor and resumed crawling.

No, Michael still was not walking, Mr. B. thought to himself, but he has improved. He never used to pull himself up onto furniture, and now he would walk if you held his hands. Michael's lack of speech development was fast becoming the B.'s greatest concern. It seemed as if everything Michael did was slower. Mr. B. wondered, When will he ever catch up?

In the past year Michael had been through many tests, more tests than Mr. B. wanted to count. He had an EEG to see if there was any brain disorder or seizure problem. That test came back normal. He had a neurological examination by a pediatric neurologist, but the doctor could not find any indication of neurological problems. Laboratory tests were run to look for imbalances within Michael's system. Once again, all the results were normal. Only the opinions of the physical therapist and speech pathologist were in agreement: developmental delay.

That thought brought a smile to Mr. B. It was the one opinion he and his wife had formed before any of the testing began. It was the one opinion they were left with after all the testing had ended.

John is a fifteen-year-old child now enrolled in a high school special education program for trainable mentally handicapped youngsters. From all outward appearances John seems to be an average high school student. His physical characteristics and motor performance are such that he could not be distinguished as different from anyone else if he were merely observed among a group of teenage boys.

At age fifteen, John is unable to read or write except for his own name. He is only able to count to seven. His social skills are estimated to be at the three- to five-year-old range; however, his social behavior within that range is inappropriate. He appears incapable of controlling his emotions, and at the slightest provocation will physically act out anger by throwing, hitting, and being generally disruptive. His attention span is extremely short (approximately five minutes), except for watching TV, which he will do for prolonged periods of time (several hours) with no emotional outbursts. His outbursts typically occur when demands are placed on him to do any functional task such as dress himself, clean his work area, or learn a simple job skill. It should be mentioned that John is able to swim and enjoys this activity. He often experiences the success of winning when competing in school meets.

John's parents became aware that he had problems at an early age when they observed that he did not crawl, walk, speak, or play with toys at the same age and in the same manner as his peers.

Several years of pursuing countless medical consultations along with extensive testing for every possible organic problem provided no answers as to the cause of John's problem. The results of his blood tests, EEG's, scans, hearing/visual tests, chromosome studies, and all other tests for anatomical or physiological abnormalities came back normal. To this day, fifteen years later, there is nothing obvious in John's family history, pre- or postnatal history, or medical makeup that can be identified as the cause of his problem.

Regardless of the diagnosis or the lack of diagnosis, we are very often asked by parents. "Have you ever seen another child who is like _____?" Whether a child has Down's syndrome, cerebral palsy, visual impairment, speech impairment, mental retardation, or any other of the many handicapping conditions, it soon becomes obvious to parents that their child is an individual. Although he may have some similarities to other children whose handicaps have or have not been given labels, each child's medical makeup, the degree or severity of his presenting problems, and the behaviors he exhibits are indeed unique in many ways.

Cerebral palsy is a prime example of a diagnosis or label that is assigned to children who exhibit a wide variety of different symptoms and problems. The diagnosis is usually made on the basis of two factors being present: 1) The child at some time—either during the birth process, immediately following birth, or at a very early age—experienced a period of time when the brain lacked oxygen, and 2) there is an obvious motor problem. Aside from these two common factors, children who are diagnosed as having cerebral palsy differ greatly from one to another. Some have hearing and/or visual problems while others do not, some have mental handicaps while others do not, some have speech problems while others do not, some have severe motor problems while others have mild motor impairments. Because of the tremendous variances between children, many doctors are beginning to avoid the practice of clumping all children who share only the two common factors of lack of oxygen and motor impairment under the single label of cerebral palsy. They prefer to diagnose each child based on specific problems (e.g., John has a speech impairment and abnormal muscle tone in his legs), thus acknowledging the differences between children.

Down's syndrome is also an example of a diagnosis within which differences exist from child to child. While all these children may have some typical physical characteristics in common, there are wide variances among them regarding their general health, intellectual capacity, and motor ability.

We find therefore that parents are constantly searching for answers to their specific questions. Most are seeking answers to questions about how their child will progress; what medical, surgical, chemical, and/or therapeutic agents will help his condition; and what degree of independence and intellect he will achieve.

Common questions asked of professionals are: Will my child walk? What mental age will he achieve? Can my deaf child go to college? How much will therapy help? Can medication or surgery alter his condition? How long will he need therapy? How long will he be in a special class?

FACTS VERSUS OPINIONS

Some parents place their trust in a single doctor even though he may not provide all of the answers they seek. Others go from doctor to doctor seeking answers. It is our experience that families whose children are diagnosed by the age of three have by that time consulted two or more doctors for various reasons. In doing so, they often run into some differing opinions. Some doctors make one diagnosis, and when the parents seek a second opinion, an entirely different diagnosis is made. Some doctors will predict the future while others will not. The frustrations felt by parents, who do not fully understand the medical aspects of the child's condition because they are not trained in the field of medicine, and the further confusion of being given conflicting information by different doctors, are problems we encounter almost daily in our work. It is understandable that parents feel extremely angered and upset by lack of or conflict within information given to them. Parents often feel that although they are not medically trained professionals, they are left no choice but to make the ultimate decisions.

Mary had been diagnosed at a year old as having hypotonia, a condition that affects muscle tone. Children with this condition have too little muscle tone and therefore do not progress at a normal rate in their motor skills. Mary was seen regularly by a pediatrician and a specialist who continued to evaluate her progress based on the diagnosis of hypotonia. Based on this diagnosis and on Mary's rate of progress, it was predicted by one doctor that she would walk by about age three. By age three Mary was not walking. In addition, her speech did not appear to be developing at a normal rate. She could say only a few single words. Her parents concluded that since she had poor muscle tone in the rest of her body, she no doubt had poor muscle tone in the muscles needed for producing speech also. The doctors agreed that this was certainly a possibility, but would not say for certain that it was so. Mary's parents agonized over the question, "Is our child not speaking because of weak muscles or is she not speaking because of other reasons?"

Her parents decided that Mary would be seen by another doctor, in the hopes that they would have their question answered. Unfortunately, the doctor they consulted not only did not answer their question, but instead confused them further. He felt that the diagnosis of hypotonia was incorrect and that the correct diagnosis was ataxia, a condition with different implications than hypotonia. Based on his diagnosis, he predicted that Mary would probably not walk until six years of age. In addition, he told Mary's parents that she had an IQ of around fifty (quite low). According to Mary's parents, his comments followed a routine medical examination of Mary, with no formal administration of IQ tests.

Extremely upset and confused, Mary's parents confronted her original doctors with the information they had been given. The original doctors said they did not agree; they still felt Mary's problems were based on their diagnosis of hypotonia.

When we talked with Mary's mother, who obviously was confused by the conflicting information, her natural response was, "I want to believe the 'better' diagnosis."

It is important to recognize that medical professionals, be they doctors or therapists, have their individual opinions and approaches. All may agree about a diagnosis, but then differ in their opinions about how to treat. Others may disagree about the diagnosis, as in Mary's case, and thus their opinions about the child's future will be different.

There are guidelines that can be used to separate medical fact from medical opinion. Medical facts are objective results obtained from formal evaluation procedures such as physical examination, or those testing procedures discussed later in this chapter. Often an accurate diagnosis can be made based on these objective results, combined with an analysis of the symptoms your child is exhibiting. For example, a child who is having frequent spasms and whose EEG is consistently abnormal would most probably be accurately diagnosed as having a seizure disorder. A child who is not responding to sound and whose audiological examination is not within normal limits would be accurately diagnosed as having a hearing impairment. Clear-cut symptoms, along with test results or facts that confirm a cause for those symptoms such as in the examples stated, lead to a diagnosis which you can be fairly certain is correct.

Opinion, however, is a conclusion that is reached based on information that is not as clear-cut and concrete. There are several areas of parental concern where medical opinion enters into the picture.

In the area of diagnosis, when a child's symptoms and/or medical problems do not fit a particular known diagnosis, where test results are either inconclusive, inconsistent, or normal, the assigning of a diagnosis by a physician can only be considered an opinion. Opinion may also play a part in determining what drugs, aides, surgical procedures, or therapies may alter the symptoms or conditions. Whether a diagnosis is based in fact or opinion, physicians often differ as regards a method of treatment. For example, some doctors believe in orthopedic bracing for children with certain motor problems, while other doctors feel that bracing has negative effects. One doctor may prefer a certain drug over another. Some doctors feel that services such as physical or speech therapy help the child reach his maximum potential, while others feel the child will be the same with or without these services. Physicians may also disagree about whether or not surgery is indicated in certain cases.

The information that parents have shared with us leads us to believe that there are differences of opinion as to the absolute treatment for any particular problem. In fact, differences of opinion in the approach to treatment appear to us to be the most common reason that parents seek second or consulting opinions.

In the case of Mary, both doctors had come to some conclusions. Their statements, however, combined fact with opinions. The conclusions were: 1) Mary was hypotonic, 2) the hypotonia was due to ataxia, 3) Mary would walk at the age of three, 4) it was possible that Mary's low tone could be responsible for delayed speech, 5) the diagnosis of hypotonia by itself was incorrect, 6) Mary would walk by the age of six, 7) Mary had a low IQ of fifty.

What is fact and what is opinion in the case of Mary is indeed confusing. The most valid conclusion given by either of the doctors is that of hypotonia, because it is something which can be felt upon examination. It was their *opinion* that she would walk at a certain age. It was their *opinion* that low tone could result in speech delays. And, because diagnostic testing was not completed, it was the *opinion* of one doctor that Mary's IQ was as low as fifty.

Probably the area in which medical professionals are most cautious about giving an opinion is predictions about a child's future. The younger the child, the more cautiously the opinion is given. Many professionals will in fact refuse to give a specific opinion about a very young child's future potential.

Beyond what objective conclusions can be drawn from test results and matching symptoms which can be regarded as facts, it can be assumed that each physician and/or medical professional from whom you seek answers and advice is providing you with their educated and best opinion.

FINDING MEDICAL SPECIALISTS

There are several ways to go about seeking the facts and opinions you need and getting the most appropriate medical treatment.

First, it is important to find a pediatrician in whom you have confidence. The pediatrician will follow your child's general development and take care of routine medical problems such as immunizations, colds, and common childhood illnesses.

Together with your pediatrician you should identify your child's special problems and symptoms. There are specialists who deal with each particular problem. Examples are as follows:

Ophthalmologist: specialist in examining and treating visual problems

Orthopedist: specialist in treating problems related to muscles and bones

Neurologist: specialist in treating problems related to the brain, spinal cord, and other nerve disorders

Cardiologist or Cardiovascular Specialist: specialist in treating problems of the heart or circulatory system

Endocrinologist: specialist in problems related to the endocrine system, where hormones are produced

Geneticist: specialist in determining hereditary factors

Psychologist: specialist (not a medical doctor) who tests overall development as it pertains to mental function

These are examples of specialists we most often encounter in the field of pediatrics. The list is far from complete. There are numerous medical specialists available to treat almost any conceivable problem.

It is our experience that most children we see are followed by a pediatrician and one or two other specialists depending on their problems. For example, a child with a motor problem may be seen by the pediatrician, orthopedist, and possibly a neurologist.

There are several ways to find the appropriate specialists who can best assess and treat your child's particular needs. Often your pediatrician will refer you to specialists in whom he has confidence and with whom he has good communication. Another source would be a facility in your community or general area that specializes in pediatrics (a children's hospital or clinic). Such a facility will most likely have the specialists you need on staff. Having several doctors in a single facility sometimes makes communication and consultation between doctors more likely.

If your child is of school age or already is receiving therapy, do not hesitate to ask his teachers or therapists to recommend doctors. Many therapists will not recommend a single doctor but are happy to furnish you with a list of hospitals, doctors, and clinics in your area.

The American Medical Association will provide names of specialists who service your area. The association is also aware of doctors who specialize in treating children and/or handicapped citizens. Such doctors often refer to themselves as pediatric neurologists, pedodontists, pediatric anesthesiologists, etc.

Parents have related to us that they feel most comfortable with recommendations that come from other parents. Parent groups, publications, and special organizations have provided many of our parents with suggestions of specialists and doctors. By receiving a recommendation in this manner, many parents expressed that they were able to get honest and frank comments about the doctor's ability and style. For some parents this appeared to eliminate part of the anxiety associated with the first visit to a new doctor.

GETTING A SECOND OPINION

Parents tell us that they are generally involved with more than one doctor, and in matters where there are conflicting opinions they seek a third or even fourth opinion (a practice with which we totally agree). Many parents also tell us that at different stages in the process of accepting their child's problem, they have been caught up in "doctor shopping," going from doctor to doctor seeking the answers they want to hear.

It is not our recommendation that you seek a third or fourth opinion simply because you disagree over a minor issue with your doctor. For example, at every visit your doctor may repeat questions to you which you find irritating. His questions may seem redundant, and you may feel as though he does not remember your child from visit to visit. This may not be the case at all; rather, your physician may be concerned that your child has changed since he last saw him. He may be watching for symptoms related to special problems or medications. Be patient—often such questions are purposefully repeated.

There have been times when we have seen families confuse acceptable medical practice with medical fads. You may read in the paper that a certain clinic has discovered the "cure" for a certain syndrome; you may see a television special that talks about a new drug that improves mental functioning; a reputable magazine may publish an article that describes the latest medical advances in controlling seizures. While such information may be true, in part or whole, it invariably is misleading. It is our belief that while it is good to follow up such articles and reports, they are not a valid reason to switch doctors or seek additional opinions.

There are times when seeking various opinions is beneficial not only to confirm a diagnosis, but to provide you with alternatives to therapy, medications, and/or surgery. For this reason, during nonemergency situations it is helpful to seek out other opinions.

Some parents find that there is much controversy in an area of medicine that directly affects their child. While medical advances are encouraging and hold out hope for many children, they can often be confusing to parents who are forced to make serious decisions regarding their child's health. If your child's medical problem falls within an area of medicine where change is taking place, it will be very difficult—if not impossible—for you, as a lay person, to keep up on all of the changes and advances. In such a situation, we encourage you to get a second opinion.

It is certainly human and natural for parents to want to believe the positive and ignore the negative when it pertains to their child, as was expressed by Mary's mother, who wanted to believe "the better diagnosis." It is our belief and the belief of many parents we see that two or more concurrent opinions provide a sufficient basis for drawing an accurate conclusion regarding diagnosis, treatment, and/ or future potential.

MEDICAL APPOINTMENTS

Each doctor you see will probably take a medical history from you to help him in assessing your child's problem. You may be given a form to fill out, or the doctor or nurse may ask you questions themselves. Common questions asked pertain to your family's health, your pregnancy, the delivery, the hospital course following the birth, your child's development (when he began to roll, crawl, walk, and talk), symptoms, problems that concern you, and medication your child takes. It would be advisable to have such information on hand so that you are able to give accurate answers. If you are not certain about any of the information, you should obtain it from your obstetrician, pediatrician, the hospital, or whatever source has your and your child's medical records. You can obtain copies of any records you need by requesting that your attending physician autho-rize them to be released to you.

When describing your child to the doctor, it is important that you tell him how you see your child without clouding issues. He will want to know exactly what your child does and does not do. This can usually be stated briefly and simply.

People often complain to us that their doctors do not listen to them. While it would certainly be ideal for every patient-doctor relationship to be on a somewhat cordial level, particularly when you are tense and nervous about your child's problem, doctors, like other people, have their unique personalities. Some have a great deal of warmth and social charm, while others are shy, abrupt, or aloof. While warmth and charm may make your visit more comfortable, the doctor who is shy, abrupt, or aloof may be excellent in his field. You cannot judge the doctor's capabilities by his social responses. If you initiate a great deal of conversation that has no specific bearing on your child's medical condition, the doctor may in fact stop listening carefully to all that you say, and may miss an important point that you wanted to convey. Knowing that his time is limited, and that he has probably set aside a specific amount of time for your appointment, try to become conscious of stating the pertinent information he will need to make an accurate medical assessment.

We suggest that you allow your doctor to guide the conversation at the beginning of the visit. Respond to his questions as simply and accurately as you can. If at the end of the examination he has not addressed all of your concerns, you should then state them and ask any questions that remain unanswered. If possible, you should prepare a written list of questions prior to your visit so that you do not forget something you wanted to ask.

It may be helpful for you to jot down notes during your visit so you can have your own record of important information you obtained from the doctor. If any medical terms are used that you do not understand, ask what they mean. As we have mentioned, the doctor's time is limited; however, you should obtain all the information that you wanted when you made the appointment.

Parents have told us it is advisable that siblings do not accompany you on a visit to the doctor. Unless there is some medical reason for them to come along, they can distract you and others in the office. Make arrangements in advance so they are cared for elsewhere when you have doctor's appointments.

COMMON TESTING PROCEDURES

If after a medical examination in the doctor's office it is determined that some form of further medical testing is needed, you will want to know certain facts regarding whatever tests are ordered: 1) Does the test require hospitalization or can it be done as an outpatient? 2) What is the doctor looking for—what answers can be obtained from the test? 3) What effect, if any, will the testing procedure have on your child, i.e., will it make him tired, irritable, etc.? 4) Is there any risk involved in the testing procedure.

The following is a list of testing procedures that appear most frequently in the medical charts of our pediatric patients, along with a very brief explanation of each.

Apgar: This is a number assigned to an infant at birth. The number indicates the overall health of the infant. Generally, the higher the number, the healthier the child.

Audiological exam: This is a hearing test, usually done by an audiologist or trained technician. It examines hearing and identifies certain types of hearing impairment.

Biopsy: This is a surgical procedure which entails removal of a small piece of tissue. This tissue is then sent to the laboratory to determine its makeup.

Brain scan: This test is administered to determine if there are any structural abnormalities in tissues of the brain. It produces pictures of the surface of the brain.

CAT scan: The initials CAT stand for Computerized Axial Tomography. This test is an in-depth study of brain structures and tissue. It produces pictures that show many layers of the brain so that the location, size, and description of abnormalities can be determined.

Cognitive testing: This assessment determines what knowledge a child has gained from his environment. It evaluates his ability to learn from his world.

EEG: The initials EEG stand for electroencephalogram. This test examines the electrical activity in the brain. It produces a picture showing waves. The size of the waves and the pattern they form determine the amount and kind of electrical activity in the brain. The test is often done to determine if seizure activity is present.

Genetic counseling: This counseling involves the study of chromosomes. It determines how certain offspring may be affected by hereditary factors.

Laboratory testing: These tests analyze the chemical makeup of the body. They aid in diagnosis by determining if body chemistry is properly balanced. Common examples are thyroid studies, amino acid determination, blood tests, urinalysis.

Neurological testing: This test examines function of the brain and other structures in the nervous system. It may involve testing of reflexes, movement, and the ability to use the basic senses. It is used to identify brain malfunction and other nerve disorders.

Ophthalmological exam: This is a vision test that examines vision as well as the anatomical structures that are involved in seeing.

Psychological exam: This evaluation assesses all areas of development, thus allowing for a total look at where a child is functioning. It may include such things as motor skills, speech, language, cognitive skills, and intellectual ability.

Physical therapy/Occupational therapy assessment: This is an evaluation that assesses motor capabilities. It looks at gross motor (legs, arms, and trunk) and fine motor (fingers, hands) performance. It determines type, quality, and functionality of movement.

Speech and language evaluation: This is an evaluation that assesses communicative abilities. Such things are examined as ability to produce and combine sounds, ability to understand and express language, and ability to use these skills in social interaction.

SUMMARY

In concluding this chapter, we feel we would be remiss if we did not call attention to the fact that aside from dealing with the initial acceptance process and apprehension about your child's future, the next most common cause of stress among the families we work with is having to deal with medical professionals. We have used such words as *confusing, angry, uneasy,* and *agonizing* in our sample case studies. These are the words parents have used in describing their experiences to us. What comes to mind when talking through these experiences with families is that throughout the course of the average person's life, probably the most difficult and stressful times are related to illness. All people feel tense, anxious, and generally upset whenever a problem arises in their lives that requires medical attention. Even when there is no problem evident, a routine medical checkup usually causes most people some anxiety.

Having a child with a handicap oftentimes necessitates more involvement with medical professionals. Along with the additional involvement comes additional responsibility to comprehend, interpret, and sort out medical information. You may need to make decisions for which you do not feel qualified. Your interpretation of information or the decision you make may tremendously affect your child's life.

Aside from the built-in stresses of scheduling appointments; sitting for hours in hospitals, clinics, and offices with an irritable, hungry, and tired child; watching your child have needles, tubes, and electrodes put in and on his body; and waiting for test results, your parental role requires yet more of you. You become, as time goes on, a very special kind of medical expert—the medical expert who can best assess how your child feels, what is bothering him, and how he responds. You best know his color, the look in his eyes, the sound of his breathing, where he hurts, and what every movement means. Almost unwittingly you learn the meaning of medical terms. Without thinking you begin to diagnose his problems. You decide what effects medications are having.

Amid the confusion, conflict, and stress, somehow almost every parent we work with has begun to or has already developed a new and special kind of courage. This courage takes the form of assertiveness in situations where before they may have felt intimidated.

Consider the suggestions in this chapter that parents have shared with us: 1) Separate facts from opinions, 2) find appropriate specialists to follow your child, 3) get several opinions in areas of conflict or confusion, 4) become familiar with medical jargon that pertains to your child, and 5) use the time you spend with medical people with whom you come in contact in the best possible way by sticking to the subject, asking questions, and taking maximum advantage of their skill and knowledge. While medical experiences are usually not pleasant, yours can be more comfortable for you.

In this medical world of fancy words, sophisticated equipment, and sterile offices, the ultimate responsibility still falls on you, the parent. What information about your child is accurate? What treatment is best? How is your child progressing? Having gathered the best information available to you, you will make the final decisions. You above anyone know your child best. You above anyone care about him most. Along with parental instinct and parental love appears to come the strength and knowledge that enables parents to make the right decisions regarding their child's health.

4. EDUCATION

PLACEMENT AND PROGRAMMING

Many parents of children with handicaps are unaware of their rights regarding the education of these children. According to law, every child between the ages of three and twenty-one years of age with a handicapping condition has a legal right to a free and appropriate education. The laws refer to all children, including those who have severe handicaps and/or medical problems.

It is important that parents of children with handicaps understand the implications of the laws regarding their education. It is impossible and impractical for our purposes to attempt to state, define, and interpret all legislation regarding the education of handicapped children. If you are interested in obtaining detailed information, you can request it from your local board of education. You can refer in particular to Public Law 94-142 and Section 504 of the Rehabilitation Act.

For our purpose, we will briefly summarize the provisions the federal government has made for the education of children with special needs.

Present legislation provides that a child with a handicapping condition can enter school at age three in a preschool or *diagnostic* program, as it is sometimes called. At age five the child enters the primary school program and continues his education through the intermediate and upper grades. He then goes on to the high school level, from which he will graduate between the ages of eighteen and twenty-one, depending on his needs. His entire education from preschool through high school is provided free of charge by the public school system.

The father of a child we had been seeing related this story to us.

I was being transferred through my job to another city. When I visited the city to which I was to move to look for housing, I figured I may as well find out what schooling would be available for my son. I phoned the board of education and told them I had a four-year-old handicapped child and wondered what types of educational programs they would have for him. They replied that they had no programs for a four-year-old, and when the child was five, they would provide special education. I then asked the person to whom I was speaking if he were aware that according to federal law they had to provide my four-year-old handicapped son with an educational program. The person said, "We are aware of the law. We just don't observe it here."

Fortunately this father is aware of his rights regarding his son's education. A parent who was not informed would have simply accepted the fact that nothing would be done.

The term *special education* is commonly used when referring to an educational setting in which services are provided for children with special needs. Because there are usually not enough of these children in a single school district to warrant a special education program, several school districts will get together and combine resources to form a special education cooperative. You can find out what cooperative would service your child by contacting your local school district.

The steps to be taken to enroll your child in a special educational program are as follows: When your child is approaching three years of age, call your school district and tell the people you have a child in need of special education. Give them your child's birth date and state that you are calling to find out what type of special education program he will be placed in at age three. Your school district may handle the matter, or the district representative may refer you to the special education cooperative to which you belong.

Prior to your child's third birthday, you should be contacted by the school system and requested to bring your child in for an observation. The purpose of the observation by the school staff is to determine what type of educational program will be appropriate for your child. This observation is sometimes referred to as diagnostic evaluation, assessment, screening, or a case study.

It should be mentioned that some states have voluntarily extended special education to include children from birth to three years of age; therefore, these states service children from birth to twenty-one years of age. To find out if your state has programs that provide services for children from birth to three, you can contact your local school district, clergy, or hospitals. These are all excellent resources to locate such programs if they exist in your area.

In addition to educational placement, the law also provides that the educational program designed for your child be appropriate in terms of his particular needs. The program should be one in which the child, regardless of his handicap, will learn, grow, and increase his independence insofar as is possible.

TERMS USED IN SPECIAL EDUCATION

With regard to your child's educational placement and programming, school educators and administrators may use many terms that are unfamiliar to you. They refer to components of the total educational process which, according to law, must be included in the planning of your child's education.

The terms *mainstreaming, least restrictive alternative, individualized educational program, related services, due process* and *nondiscriminatory testing* are among the most common you will probably hear. You should have some knowledge of these terms and understand how they might apply to your child.

Mainstreaming/Least Restrictive Alternative

Some children's handicapping condition may interfere only in certain areas of learning. In other areas the child may function normally or even excel. For classes in which the handicapping condition does not interfere with the learning process, children should be integrated with nonhandicapped children. They should be separated only for classes in which specialized educational methods must be used because of the handicapping condition. This concept in education is referred to as *mainstreaming*. Mainstreaming provides the opportunity for children to develop social skills and gain emotional maturity. These benefits apply to both the handicapped child and the nonhandicapped child.

There are some people, however, who think that mainstreaming places the child with special needs at a disadvantage. They think that the child who moves about slowly or who needs any special assistance with daily activities, such as dressing or eating, is at an educational and social disadvantage in a classroom with nonhandicapped children.

There are numerous placement alternatives in addition to mainstreaming. The various alternatives allow for the tremendous differences in the type and severity of handicapping condition. Children are grouped according to their similarities in what are termed *self-contained classrooms*. Children within these classrooms usually function at or near the same level mentally and physically. The ratio of teachers and aides to children is usually low. Placement in a self-contained classroom is based on the child's mental and physical abilities. With regard to such placement, you may hear labels such as: *PH, MH, EMH, TMH, LD,* and *EDBD* applied to your child. These abbreviations for descriptive terms will be discussed in Chapter 6.

The goal of all educational programs for handicapped children is to provide a curriculum that parallels educational programs of nonhandicapped children. It also attempts to provide your handicapped child with exposure to nonhandicapped children as much as possible in an academic setting. These goals constitute the concept of *least restrictive alternative*. That is, each child's educational needs are examined. The program that most clearly parallels the program of a nonhandicapped child is judged to be least restricting. Parents and educators must decide together what educational placement is least restricting in the case of each individual child.

Individualized Educational Program (IEP)

The term *IEP* (individualized educational program) refers to a written document which is prepared for each individual child each year, describing that child's educational program. Contained in the IEP are specific goals for the year and a description of how these goals will be achieved. As goals are achieved, the IEP is revised and new goals are set. Most schools review a child's IEP with his parents annually. The IEP, therefore, provides a means whereby the child's individual program plan can be examined and his progress can be documented, and gives parents a point of reference regarding the child's skills.

Related Services

The term *related services* refers to services apart from those provided in the classroom that may benefit your child. This would include such services as those provided by a physical therapist (PT), occupational therapist (OT), speech and language pathologist, visually impaired specialist or hearing impaired educator. The amount of related services a child receives would depend on the results of evaluations. Such evaluations also determine how often such services are needed and how long each session should last. Some children tolerate one hourly session per week, while others do better with three 20-minute sessions per week. Related services are a part of the child's IEP so that plans, progress, and levels of function in the areas in which he is receiving related services can also be reviewed.

Nondiscriminatory Testing

All children are entitled to *nondiscriminatory testing*. This means that all factors that would affect a child's ability to perform on a test must be considered and appropriate adjustments made in the testing and/or scoring procedure. Such factors may include a bilingual home environment, the child's socioeconomic status, or a visual, hearing, or physical impairment. Any of these factors may influence the speed or accuracy of the testing procedure and must be considered.

Due Process

In explaining the term *due process,* it is important first that you understand something about the complexity of the legislation regarding special education. It is not quite so simple as it may seem. The laws are extremely complicated and there is a great deal of room for interpretation. While an understanding of the overall complexity of the situation is not meant to deter you from seeking a totally appropriate educational placement for your handicapped child, you should be aware that you may encounter some confusion in the way the law is interpreted in different areas and by different people. You should also be aware that such factors as time, money, and increased enrollment may have a bearing on whether an educational facility is in fact able to provide what you consider to be the ideal amount and kind of service for your child. One final consideration would be how your child may affect other children in a specific setting you may prefer. For example, you may feel your child should be mainstreamed, but he may be extremely disruptive and affect the education of other children in a regular classroom.

If, after considering all the facts involved, you think that you wish to question your child's educational program in some way, your first step would be to voice your concerns to the school representative. An ideal time to do so would be at the placement conference or the yearly review. Usually an agreement can be reached without going further than this step. If, however, an agreement cannot be reached, and you strongly think that your child is not benefiting from the program provided for him, you may challenge his program by going through a procedure referred to as *due process*. This involves a meeting between the parents and the school with an impartial hearing officer present. This officer hears both sides of the disagreement and gives a final recommendation to the local educational agency. If a due process hearing becomes necessary, your school district will provide you with information about the procedure.

SUMMARY

In summary, the important questions to be answered regarding your child's educational placement and program are: 1) Is he in a setting where his limitations are understood and his strengths are built upon? 2) Has an individual educational program been designed for your child that sets realistic goals, explains how those goals are to be reached, and describes your child accurately? 3) Is your child receiving the related services that will aid him in the learning process and/or increase his independence? 4) Do the tests administered to your child reflect an accurate picture of the level at which you see him functioning? If answers to these questions are positive, your child's educational placement and program are probably appropriate.

SCHOOL RECORDS

Legislation regarding education also refers to the accessibility and confidentiality of the school records. Your child's school record or file contains several things. It would include all notes and reports written by school personnel (teachers, nurses, etc.), all your child's IEP's, evaluations and test results, and all information about your child that has been accumulated since he entered the public school system. In addition to the data obtained from school personnel, the file may also include reports obtained from sources outside the school, such as physicians, hospitals, or clinics.

It is important to note here that no information about your child can be obtained from an outside source without your written permission. Also, no records on your child can be sent from the school to an outside source without your written permission. The only way information contained in the file can be shared without your signed approval is among personnel within the public school system. This exception is made because it is assumed that such sharing is for the sole purpose of benefiting your child.

You may request copies of any portion of your child's file that contains information obtained directly from school personnel. If, however, you desire a copy of a report that was obtained from an outside source, you must request it from the original source (physician, hospital, etc.). The school can show such a report to you in the file but cannot copy it and pass it on to you.

You may see your child's file at any time and, in fact, have input into what is contained in it. For example, if a particular evaluation appears to misrepresent your child's level of functioning as you see it, a note can be inserted to that effect: "Mrs. X stated that the portion of the report indicating that Johnny has only ten words in his vocabulary is incorrect. Mrs. X reports that Johnny has at least twenty words he says at home consistently." Such input is important in the case of a child who performs differently at home from the way he does in school.

It is a good idea to develop your own personal file about your child. It can include your personal notes about his development, copies of what is contained in the school file, and other pertinent medical information. Many parents have found it beneficial to make notes of the amount of radiation exposure their child has had, medications their child has received at any given time, and the effects of such medication on their child. This file may expedite matters should you move or change schools or doctors. It will also help you to follow your child's progress and prepare you to suggest ideas for educational programming.

THE PARENTAL ROLE IN PUBLIC EDUCATION

During the years your child is enrolled in the public school system, you will be called upon many times to participate in the planning of his education. This participation is usually in the format of a meeting or conference. The meeting/conference may be for the purpose of enrolling into a program, reviewing or revising the IEP, discussing placement, or working out a specific problem. Many professionals may be present, or a single educator may request a meeting with you. Following these encounters with the school, parents have shared various reactions with us. Some have said they felt uncomfortable in the presence of so many professionals. Many have not understood the terminology used. Sometimes questions have been left unanswered or an important point has been omitted.

It is our experience that meetings between school personnel and parents are most productive and satisfying when parents come to them prepared and knowledgeable. In order to do so, we suggest that you determine the purpose of the meeting beforehand, become familiar with the terminology we have defined, review or bring your personal file, and prepare questions pertinent to the meeting. If it is appropriate that a person who is not part of the public school system but is involved with your child have input into the meeting, you can request that he be invited. You may want to take notes during the meeting. These notes can be added to your personal file, shared with family members who are not present, or shared with your physician.

The parental role in education may vary, depending on the type of facility in which your child is enrolled, whether it is a public or a private facility, whether it is residential, and, of course, on your child's ability to assume responsibility for his own educational needs. In any case, your ideas and thoughts are vital to enriching your child's educational environment.

5. SPECIAL TEACHERS AND THERAPISTS

YOUR ROLE IN THERAPY

It should be obvious that no amount of therapy and/or education will be of value in helping your child reach his maximum potential unless you provide carry-over in the home on a daily basis.

One, two, or three hours a week of intensive therapy is useless if, during the times between sessions, the child is not managed correctly. For this reason, the parental role in therapy is critical.

Your presence during therapy sessions should serve to make you an active part of your child's therapy. In many hospitals and agencies (UCP, Easter Seals, etc.) parents are present during the treatment sessions. The same is also true of private therapy. The treatment sessions where you are present should be divided so that part of the time you are observing. During this time it is important that you remain quiet. It may even be necessary to remain out of sight so that you do not distract your child from the therapeutic tasks. The other part of the session should be devoted to teaching you what you should be doing at home with your child to reinforce specific skills. During this time you should be actively involved in trying the techniques you are learning with the professional present so you can be certain you are doing them correctly.

If your child is receiving all his special services in school it will be impossible for you to be present at every therapy session. It is up to you, however, to make arrangements to observe treatments periodically to find out what you should be doing at home and to make certain you are notified when changes are made in your child's treatment plan. Many school educators keep close contact with parents either through note writing or by phone. It is likely that they would welcome calls or notes from you also. It will be up to you to make sure you have enough contact with the school to follow your child's progress and do things at home to reinforce what he is learning in school.

We have found that the parent is the child's best and most natural therapist. While this is true, you must also remember that you are a mother or father. That is, you should not feel that you must spend twenty-four hours a day being your child's therapist.

Just as your child may be in need of special exercises, equipment, etc., so too is he in need of parenting. Time spent cuddling, holding, and just plain loving your child is probably the most important time you spend with him. Many therapeutic techniques can fit into daily care and can be carried out during dressing, bathing, feeding, and playtime activities. In this way such activities are not only functional but are also very natural. You can provide your child with cuddles, hugs, and love along with therapeutic exercises.

If it is necessary to set aside time to do exercises or work on specific tasks, decide on a set time period each day for that purpose. If at all possible it should be the same time every day, and a limit should be set on how long it will last each day. In other words, therapy time should be a structured part of your and your child's daily routine. The child who knows that he is going to work on something will put forth greater effort if he is aware that he will be finished within a certain period of time. You as a parent will also be more enthusiastic and put more into a session with a child when time limits are set. If your therapy activities are left unscheduled, you may do a haphazard job of fitting in an exercise or task here and there, never feeling you have done enough.

Once you are getting your child all the specialized professional help he needs, and you are spending constructive time with him at home, you can feel assured that you are doing all you can, both medically and educationally, for your child. Your parental role in therapy and education for your child need not be overwhelming to you or to your child. It can be considered a necessary and matter-of-fact part of your total parent-child relationship, allowing plenty of time for the things that all parents and children do together as well as those which they do apart.

WHEN TO BEGIN THERAPY

When do you begin therapy? Probably the best answer to this question is whenever you find out that your child has special needs. The accent within education today falls strongly on early intervention and stimulation. "Early" can be defined chronologically (as in programs from birth to three years old), or it can be defined in terms of when the need for services is discovered.

The "wait and see" approach, while still around, has found little support lately. Doctors, therapists, and educators alike advocate a prompt-treatment approach. Such an approach utilizes your child's critical periods of development (early childhood, soon after traumatic injuries, immediately following strokes, etc.).

TEACHERS

Special Education Teachers
The teachers your child has throughout his school years are likely to have a profound effect on his life. Special education teachers function in much the same way as regular classroom teachers. The major difference between them lies in teaching methods (how they teach) and curriculum (what they teach).

Unlike therapists or those professionals who provide related and consultative services, the special education teacher provides for the child's overall development in a classroom setting. This may include teaching such skills as self-help (eating, dressing, toileting, etc.), social development, and physical development. In an effort to provide such a wide scope of services, special education teachers will often work with therapists and consultants, attempting to integrate specific skills into everyday experiences.

All special education teachers are certified in specific areas. To be certified in an area, a teacher is required to take a certain number of classes that deal with a handicapping condition; he or she must also work as a student teacher with children who exhibit that handicap.

Areas of certification are broken down according to disabilities that children exhibit. For example, a teacher may be certified in teaching the mentally handicapped, learning disabled, emotionally disturbed, physically handicapped, or multiple handicapped. Teachers are often required to have certain types of certification to work with certain types of handicapping conditions because the techniques used in a classroom will depend upon the special needs of the children in that classroom.

Resource teachers

A resource teacher provides special education services on a regular basis; however, these services are not provided within the classroom setting. Some resource teachers provide services for individual students who require special help only in specific areas of learning. For example, if a child is doing well in all other areas of schoolwork, but continues to show difficulty in the area of math, he may receive additional help in this area from a resource teacher.

These teachers, like special education teachers, have received training in various areas of special education. A child in need of special help may go to a resource room regularly and receive this help. Along with this individual instruction, the resource teacher coordinates efforts with the classroom teacher, thus providing the child with a total program.

Consultants

The definition of what a consultant is varies widely from program to program. Some consultants only work with teachers in regular classes. Others work with special education teachers. Some only aid a teacher in the diagnosis of a child's problem; others will also help a teacher plan and initiate a child's program. If a consultant is involved in your child's program, it is probably best if you ask for a definition of his role.

Consultants generally aid teachers in defining and intervening with a specific problem a child may have. They may see your child directly for a few sessions and then, along with your child's teacher, determine the best programming. After the initial program has been determined, the consultant is likely to monitor or check up on your child's progress in the program.

Another way in which a consultant functions is by training teachers how to do specific techniques. This training (sometimes referred to as in-service training) usually takes place after school hours or on special days allotted by the school district or program director.

Consultants are usually special education teachers who receive additional training or have specific skills in particular therapeutic techniques. Sometimes a teacher who has simply had more experience will act as a consultant to another teacher. Recently therapists (occupational, physical, etc.) have also begun to act as consultants for teachers.

Itinerant Teachers

Many handicapping conditions are termed low-incidence conditions; they do not occur as frequently as other handicapping conditions. Examples of these conditions are deafness and blindness. It is sometimes not possible to service these children in special classes or programs because there are not enough students to constitute a program. When this occurs, an *itinerant teacher* is usually hired and itinerant services are begun.

Itinerant teachers travel from place to place, providing special programming for those children in need. Itinerants are used in cases where there are not enough children to constitute a whole program (such as in low-incidence handicapping conditions) and in rural areas where there are not enough children within a given area to constitute a program.

Teacher Aides/Therapy Aides

These paraprofessionals—assistants to professionals—work closely with teachers and therapists. Their work includes preparing special materials, following specific lessons written by a teacher, and giving general assistance to the classroom teacher. While some aides lack the educational experience a teacher has, many are nonetheless excellent educators in the classroom.

Aides are usually provided with a great deal of in-service training from the teacher as well as from other professionals within a school setting. Many work directly with students on specific tasks set up by the teacher. In this way it is possible to provide individual assistance for children within a classroom setting.

THERAPISTS

Therapists are specially trained professionals who attempt to correct or minimize the negative aspects of a handicapping condition. Similar to special education teachers, they often have areas of expertise. For example, a physical therapist may elect to specialize in pediatrics, heart conditions, or stroke patients. This would not necessarily mean that they are not qualified to work in other areas of physical therapy, but that their case load consists predominantly of one type of patient.

In the school system, therapists are often referred to as *related services*. Such services are provided to support the therapy taking place in the classroom. Supportive services may involve direct (weekly, biweekly, etc.) therapy, or they may involve the therapist consulting with the classroom teacher on specific activities.

In an adult workshop or educational setting this same type of arrangement may take place. Needs of the handicapped adult are often different from those of a child, and for this reason the intensity of therapy as well as the goals of therapy may change from setting to setting.

The therapist who would treat your child would specialize in the discipline related to your child's needs. The following therapists are most commonly found in school and workshop facilities.

Physical Therapists

The physical therapist (PT) works with any child with a motor impairment or motor delay. The motor problem may be due to a physical handicap, mental handicap, visual impairment, or any one of the many other conditions that affect a child's ability to move about the environment normally. A physical therapist is capable of implementing a program based on the physician's diagnosis. This program may include such things as specific exercises, positioning, and/or general recommendations with respect to movement.

In order to work with your child, a physical therapist must receive a prescription from your child's physician. Obtaining a prescription at a routine office visit can sometimes facilitate the onset of services. Prescriptions are often limited to specified time periods. For example, your prescription may be good for six months or one year. For this reason your therapist may ask to receive a new prescription periodically.

Occupational Therapists

An occupational therapist (OT) works with any child whose ability to use objects in his environment is impaired. This problem may stem from any type of motor impairment, visual impairment, or damage that affects the child's ability to receive information from his environment.

Techniques used in pediatric treatment by physical and occupational therapists are often similar, since the emphasis in both disciplines is on developing motor skills that will enable the child to move about in and manipulate his environment. In many pediatric settings your child may see either the PT or the OT.

Occupational therapists are often employed by rehabilitation programs to improve vocational as well as physical skills. Such treatment attempts to foster independence by finding adaptive or alternative skills. Occupational therapists who function with re-habilitation programs often work closely with vocational trainers and evaluators. Ultimately their goals are geared toward more indepen-dent living and working conditions.

Like physical therapists, occupational therapists may be required to obtain a prescription from a doctor in order to evaluate or treat a patient.

Speech and Language Therapists

The speech and language therapist works with children who are exhibiting delays or difficulties in communicating. These prob-lems may be in one or several areas of speech and language development. Since communication is essential in the total education process, children who have difficulties in this area often suffer serious disadvantages. The speech and language therapist works to provide a communication system for children by stimulating or intervening in the process of speech and language acquisition.

Developmental Therapists

The term *developmental therapist* may or may not be familiar to you, depending upon where you live and the type of educational setting your child is in. This therapist acts as a teacher does in many ways. The therapist works with any child who is exhibiting delays or difficulties in performing skills that are appropriate for his age. The lack of performance may be due to delays, social/emotional prob-lems, visual impairments, or any one of the number of educational problems children exhibit.

PSYCHOLOGISTS

The psychologist may be involved in doing diagnostic testing that aids in determining educational needs for children who have various handicapping conditions. These tests help in deciding upon the child's classroom placement, related services to be offered, and specific educational techniques that may improve learning.

Aside from administering tests, psychologists often work with families to help with problems in home management. These problems may be related to behavioral management, social and/or emotional adjustment.

Many psychologists actively participate in a child's educational planning and would be very willing to explain testing and recommendations to parents as well as teachers.

SOCIAL SERVICE PROFESSIONALS

Social service professionals perform a wide variety of services, including counseling children, parents, and families; gathering necessary information for parents; consulting with teachers and therapists; and working as a client or child advocate. The services of these professionals widely vary and are often dependent upon the individual professional's expertise and educational background, the population which is being served, and the type of setting within which they are functioning.

Many of our parents have found an invaluable friend and asset in the social service professional who services their program. These professionals are often willing to develop new parent groups or programs if they are made aware of the need for them. Often social service professionals seek out new ways in which to service parents and families. Many are very receptive to new ideas from parents.

Social workers can also help you to find sources for assistance that you or your child may need. They are usually aware of public-assistance policies as well as many private funds available to parents and children.

Social service professionals use various titles to identify themselves. Such titles may include the following: social workers, counselors, case workers, case managers, support service professionals, and mental health professionals.

ADULT PROGRAMS

Supervisors/Therapists/Teachers

Special programs and workshops that meet the needs of handicapped adults provide the services of supervisors, therapists, and teachers in many ways. Some programs are educationally based;

other programs are vocationally geared. The services your child receives in an adult program will depend on whether his needs are primarily educational or vocational.

Some programs hire certified special education teachers to act as supervisors. Other agencies require little or no special educational training for these positions. The former setting may expect special education teachers to learn vocational jobs in order to train the clients; the latter may expect supervisors knowledgeable in a particular vocation to learn special education techniques in order to teach clients job skills. Adult programs may also employ consultants to work with supervisors. Consultants are used in workshops similarly to the way in which consulting teachers discussed earlier are used in the classroom.

Vocational Evaluators

A vocational evaluator's primary job is to test and determine an individual's strengths and weaknesses in relation to job skills. These evaluators use a variety of measures to determine what may be an individual's aptitude and ability to pursue a certain career. Such determinations are usually made from tests administered (objective data) and an interview with the client (subjective data). It is common for evaluators to take this information and then counsel the client on job acquisition or job training.

Evaluations of this type are likely to occur when an adolescent or adult is attempting to enter or reenter the job market. Vocational evaluators commonly work with a team of professionals within a rehabilitation setting. Through the team effort, total career counseling is provided for many handicapped citizens.

Activity Therapists

Activity therapists use recreational activities to achieve therapeutic goals. These activities may include such things as crafts, music, dance, and athletics. Recreational activities not only foster skill development, but more importantly, provide appropriate social situations to develop such skills. Given this atmosphere, clients learn to appropriately use specific skills in a social setting.

6. EDUCATIONAL AND MEDICAL TERMS AND DIAGNOSES

Parents have related to us that they are often confused by labels and terms used to describe their children. This usually occurs in connection with the children's educational placement and the need for related services. Terms and labels are also used in a clinical or medical setting with regard to diagnosis and treatment.

It is not our purpose, nor are we qualified, to discuss specific diagnoses. We can, however, provide some general information about the following common terms and labels which you may encounter in the course of your child's medical treatment and educational process.

Physical Handicap (PH)
Development Delay (DD)
Multiple Handicap (MH)
Mental Handicap (EMH, TMH, Severe and Profound)
Learning Disability (LD)
Emotionally Disturbed/Behaviorally Disordered (ED/BD)
Speech and Language Impairment
Visual Impairment
Hearing Impairment
Anomalies
Progressive and Degenerative Disorders

Although many listed may not apply to your child, we encourage you to become familiar with them so that your overall knowledge of various handicapping conditions and educational terminology increases, along with your ability to relate to other parents and educators who are involved in meeting the special needs of children.

PHYSICAL HANDICAP

A physical handicap is a condition that limits one's physical capabilities. The condition may be severely limiting, such as paralysis in both legs, or it may be a mildly limiting condition such as weakness in one arm.

Conditions we commonly see in children that result in a physical handicap are related to problems in the muscular system, the central nervous system (brain and spinal cord), or physical deformities. If the condition only affects the child's physical performance, and he appears to be functioning normally in all other areas of development, the diagnosis is termed a physical handicap (PH).

Signs and symptoms of a physical handicap are usually easy to detect. The child is either not moving or is having difficulty moving normally. His muscles may feel too tight when you try to move him, or they may feel too floppy. He may lie or sit in odd positions. He may use only one side of his body and not the other. A parent or caretaker will usually notice these types of symptoms in the day-to-day care of the child. As soon as a problem is noticed or suspected, the child should be seen for a medical evaluation.

The diagnosis of a physical handicap can be made by a pediatrician. In most cases, depending on the nature of the handicap, the pediatrician will refer you to a specialist who deals with physical handicaps—usually an orthopedist, a neurologist, or a physiatrist, who will confirm the diagnosis.

Following the diagnosis, treatment should begin. Some physical handicaps can be helped with drug therapy (medication). In addition to medication, other forms of therapy are often suggested that will help the child reach his maximum potential. Professionals who treat children with physical handicaps are physical therapists (PT's) and occupational therapists (OT's). The PT and/or OT will work with your child to teach him to function as normally as possible and achieve his maximum level of independence. There are also surgical and/or bracing techniques that are effective in the treatment of certain physical handicaps. The need for surgery or bracing requires careful consideration on the part of doctors, therapists, and parents to determine the long-term effects it will have on the child's ability to function more normally.

Examples of conditions that could fall into the category of physical handicaps are cerebral palsy (ataxic, athetoid, spastic, or mixed), spina bifida, hypotonicity, hypertonicity, juvenile rheumatoid arthritis, hemiplegia, hemipareses, cerebral vascular accident (stroke), Werdnig-Hoffman disease, Tay-Sachs disease, and other syndromes or diseases where motor function is affected.

DEVELOPMENTAL DELAY

A child is said to have a developmental delay (DD) when he is achieving the normal developmental milestones (rolling, sitting, crawling, and walking), but at a later age than is normally expected. For example, a child who learns to roll over at six months old, learns to sit at ten months old, and learns to walk at two years old would be described as a child with a developmental delay, since most children roll by about four months, sit by about seven months, and walk by about fifteen months old.

The signs of a developmental delay are simply that the child is not achieving developmental milestones at an expected age. It should be noted, however, that parents should not panic if a child has not achieved a certain milestone by a certain age; for example, if by eleven months old a child is not crawling, but he did roll and sit at the appropriate age. Some children will skip over a stage of development for one reason or another and go on to the next stage. The developmentally delayed child is late in every stage of development. When he does achieve a skill, he performs it in a normal manner.

We have cited examples of motor delays. A developmentally delayed child, however, may be delayed in the area of speech and language, cognition, and/or social emotional growth.

The diagnosis of a developmental delay is made by the pediatrician and is based on what he sees the child doing, as well as your reports on what he is doing at different ages. When you go for routine checkups you will usually be questioned by the doctor about your child's development. You should describe what your child is doing and when he began doing it as accurately as possible. Raise any concerns you have about his development.

Some premature babies exhibit a developmental delay up to a certain age and then catch up with their peers. In the case of premature babies, doctors often refer to a *gestational* and a *chronological* age. The gestational age refers to the age the child would be if he had been a full-term baby. The chronological age refers to the child's age based on his actual birth date. In other words, a child born in June who was two months premature would, in December, have a gestational age of four months and chronological age of six months. Developmental progress is then based on the baby's gestational age, since it is felt that he still needs to make up for the two months that he lacked in utero.

When the diagnosis of a developmental delay is made the pediatrician may refer you to a specialist (usually a neurologist) to rule out the possibility of the delay being related to any brain or nerve damage. Tests such as the CAT scan or EEG may be needed to rule out this possibility.

If all test results are normal, the treatment of choice, if available, would be overall developmental stimulation. This can be provided by a therapist or teacher who is trained in special education and/or child development. Parents may be taught techniques and given ideas by doctors, teachers, or therapists to stimulate development during daily activities in the home.

MULTIPLE HANDICAP

A multiple handicap (MH) is diagnosed when a child has more than one handicapping condition. The severity of the handicapping conditions may vary from mild to severe. For example, a child may be both severely physically and mentally handicapped, or he may be severely physically and mildly mentally handicapped. Any combination of handicapping conditions may exist, with variances in the degree to which physical, mental, and social function are influenced.

The signs of various handicaps are discussed under their separate headings. Obviously the child who shows signs of having several handicapping conditions should be seen for medical evaluation.

The term *multiply handicapped* is usually not used when making a medical diagnosis. It is more often used to describe a child for educational placement. The medical diagnosis would be stated as the problem that caused the handicapping conditions, such as cerebral palsy, in which there may be more than one handicapping condition.

The pediatrician who has made the medical diagnosis would usually refer you to specialists who treat the types of handicapping conditions your child exhibits.

Treatment for multiple handicaps may include some medication or surgery, depending on which medical problem has been identified. Further treatment would depend on the combination of handicaps—it may include physical therapy, occupational therapy, speech and language therapy, visual training, auditory training, or special education classes. Such services can help your child achieve his maximum potential in all areas of development.

MENTAL HANDICAP

In some areas the term *retardation* continues to be favored over *mentally handicapped*. Children labeled either mentally retarded or handicapped exhibit marked delays in such areas as thinking, speaking, self-help, social-emotional and motoric skills.

There are some behavioral characteristics often associated with children who have mental handicaps. They are slow or delayed in all areas of development. They do not exhibit marked strengths in any single area; skills are generally depressed. They learn much slower than other children. They need continuous exposure to experiences as well as repetition in their lives to achieve competence in any given task. At times they may plateau or fail to continually improve their skills. These children may appear to be less spontaneous and less enthusiastic during their first few years of life. You may notice they are not creative in their play, but rather play with their toys repetitively in the same way. They may not be able to play well alone. They may be slow in walking or talking. They may have poor coordination.

There are some medical conditions that are often associated with mental handicap. Examples include Down's syndrome, some types of cerebral palsy, seizure disorder, and brain tissue abnormalities. These associations may or may not be accurate in every case, and we urge you to obtain adequate assessment information and counseling to enable you to fully understand your child's diagnosis (see Chapter 3).

The diagnosis of a mental handicap may be given to you by your doctor. Oftentimes it is determined from certain medical tests. These tests may include an EEG, CAT scan, and neurological exam. Tests should be complemented with an educational assessment to estimate the learning capabilities of your child. Such assessments include a set or battery of tests, an interview with the child, and a review of his total background. The battery should take into consideration your child's age, socioeconomic background, physical capabilities, and approximate level of achievement.

Mental handicap is primarily viewed by educators in terms of the child's learning potential. The terms *trainable mentally handicapped* (TMH), *educable mentally handicapped* (EMH), *severe, profound, moderate,* and *mild* are used by educators to describe levels of mental handicaps.

Treatment for mental handicap is provided by a special educator. Some related services such as occupational or speech therapy may be included in the school program. The type of tasks your child will work at in school, the time required to achieve competency in a task, and the overall quality with which he will be able to perform the task will depend on his individual learning capabilities.

Because mentally handicapped children progress slowly, activities need to be repeated often or scheduled into a routine. They need exposure to different ways to learn the same concept. Skills need to be broken down into small steps so that they can master a task a little at a time. School experiences for severely and profoundly handicapped children may center around activities such as gaining understanding about their bodies through positioning them in different ways, and using vision and hearing to increase general awareness of their surroundings.

A mental handicap is a permanent disability in that the child will always need assistance to learn new tasks and new responsibilities. An early and appropriate education is geared toward developing educational skills and training for independence.

LEARNING DISABILITY

Children with learning disabilities have difficulty in acquiring new skills. The difficulty may be in the area of thinking, listening, speaking, understanding, writing, reading, spelling, and/or arithmetic. They may be awkward in their motor skills. While their intelligence is average or above average, these children continue to demonstrate difficulties. Children with learning disabilities may evidence many areas of strength and only one area of weakness, or they may evidence a few areas of weakness and several areas of strength.

In general, a child with learning disabilities is one who 1) has average or above average intelligence, 2) has adequate vision and hearing, and 3) is achieving considerably less than what might be expected of him educationally.

Along with the characteristics listed in the above definition, a child may exhibit none, one, or many of the following characteristics: He may have a short attention span. He may become interested in one toy or activity for very short periods of time, changing activities frequently throughout the day. It may appear that he has difficulty focusing on any given activity. These children are sometimes described as "very active" and "always moving." They may find it difficult to sit still for any period of time. They may repeat certain actions again and again without obvious purpose or result.

Sometimes these children appear to have difficulty remembering what was heard or seen. They may be unable to repeat back names or numbers correctly. They may be unable to recall what they saw on their way to school or what they have seen on a trip to the zoo. These problems in memory can make learning a much more difficult experience for them.

Sometimes these children may experience perceptual problems. These are problems in determining differences between and similarities within the things children hear and see. As we have already said, these problems are not in their ability to see or hear, but rather in the way the senses receive and understand information in the environment. For example, a child who has difficulty distinguishing circles from squares or seeing the difference between a *d* and a *b* would be described as having a perceptual difficulty.

A psychological and an educational assessment combined may determine if your child has a learning disability, as well as what area(s) are affected. Such assessments are administered by a psychologist or diagnostician trained in the various testing procedures used with children. The test results will help to determine the best educational curriculum for your child.

The effect a learning disability has on a child's skills could range from mild to severe. Likewise, their schooling may range from occasionally being seen by a special teacher to being in a special class all day long (self-contained classroom). Teachers who are specially trained in the field of learning disabilities will help your child learn in a way that is best for him.

Examples of conditions that fall into the category of learning disabilities are hyperactivity, perceptual problems, processing problems, and visual motor problems.

EMOTIONALLY DISTURBED/BEHAVIORALLY DISORDERED (ED/BD)

A child is said to be emotionally disturbed/behaviorally disordered when he is, in the opinion of medical and/or educational professionals, not relating appropriately to the environment. These children are often unable to build or maintain relationships with their families, peers, or teachers. Often symptoms of depression and unrealistic fears are associated with this condition.

The severity and symptoms of this condition vary widely. At the one extreme a child may appear to totally tune out all objects and people in his environment. At the other extreme, he may use objects incorrectly and relate to people improperly. In either case the child's emotional responses and behavior are considered abnormal, thus the term emotionally disturbed/behaviorally disordered.

The diagnosis of emotionally disturbed/behaviorally disordered is a difficult one to make. Often many years pass before a physician, psychologist, or parent will conclude that it is in fact the child's problem. The diagnosis is difficult for several reasons. Children who are not functioning normally and do not appear to have any visible medical conditions that could be the cause of inappropriate behavior need to be tested extensively to rule out medical conditions that could be the cause of this inappropriate behavior. It is thought that medical conditions such as severe chemical imbalances in the body can result in behavioral changes. An example of this is Tourette's syndrome. Once this syndrome is identified it can usually be treated with medication.

Following a medical workup, psychological testing is often administered. The test results may or may not be conclusive. To identify ED/BD problems, one must first eliminate other possible factors and secondly establish the existence of emotional and behavioral problems through psychological testing.

It is often a long and tedious process. While factors are being eliminated and conclusive testing is being conducted, parents are most often in an agonizing state, wondering what could possibly be wrong with their child. When a diagnosis is made, it is usually done by a team of people: a neurologist, psychologist, or psychiatrist; an educator; and the parents.

At this point many parents ask what caused this problem. Most often the answer is not known. There are cases where a child is abused or neglected, or where he has endured a severe traumatic experience. In such cases the cause of the disorder can be assumed.

In the case of the child who comes from the average home, however, it may be assumed that there are causes for this problem that we cannot identify.

There are many approaches to the treatment of ED/BD children. Depending on the severity and nature of the problem, some approaches are successful. There are some children who do not respond to treatment programs as successfully as others. Treatment approaches commonly involve educational techniques and various medications.

The professionals involved in the treatment of ED/BD children may include a psychologist, psychiatrist, special educator, and speech pathologist. Recently occupational and physical therapists have become interested in the treatment of these children.

There are facilities that specialize in the treatment of ED/BD children. Some feel that temporary removal from the home and placement in a protected environment is most effective. Others believe that the daily school setting, while living at home and working with the family, is equally effective. Such a decision will have to be made by you. The team of professionals involved in the treatment and care of your child, along with the social worker who can provide information about various facilities, can help you in your decision—but your decision should ultimately be based on the needs of your child and your family.

Examples of conditions that fall into the category of emotionally disturbed/behaviorally disordered are: schizophrenia, autism, psychosis, neurosis, and phobias.

SPEECH AND LANGUAGE IMPAIRMENT

A child who has difficulty communicating, is said to have a speech and language impairment. The problem may stem for an inability to produce and coordinate sounds (speech disorders), or from problems in using speech in order to communicate (language disorders).

Many parents think of speech disorders as problems in sound production (articulation disorders). Parents are familiar with children who lisp or substitute sounds. Such articulation problems certainly are one type of speech disorder, but there are also many others. A child may have difficulty coordinating speech sounds. He may be unable to breathe correctly in order to say long patterns of sounds. He may be unable to control any one of a number of functions necessary for speech.

A language problem develops when a child has difficulty 1) in understanding or comprehending (receptive language), or 2) in putting into words what he understands (expressive language).

There are many reasons why a child develops language disorders and delays. Some children develop the skills that are necessary for speech and language, but at a much slower rate. Other children cannot seem to develop these skills naturally.

Parents usually first notice speech and language problems when their child is young. They observe that he is not talking as much or as well as he should. Sometimes problems are not detected until later, when the child enters school. At this time teachers or therapists may recognize that a child has intelligibility or grammatical problems.

Communication disorders are diagnosed by a speech and language pathologist/therapist. Depending upon the impairment your child has, the therapist will determine what problem exists, what may have caused the problem, and the appropriate treatment for the disorder. The therapist may need to consult with your child's doctor or teacher in order to provide you with complete information regarding your child's impairment.

Speech and language impairments are usually treated through therapy. There are some organic disorders or structural disorders such as cleft palate or vocal nodules that respond successfully to surgery or prosthetic devices. The implementation of therapy or surgery to correct speech and language problems will be based upon your child's needs and diagnosis.

Speech and language provide children with communication skills necessary to develop and mature other skills. Such areas as cognitive, social, and emotional development are all based upon the acquisition of speech and language skills. It is an important and integral part of your child's overall development.

Examples of conditions that fall into the category of speech and language impairments include apraxia, dysarthria, and aphasia.

HEARING IMPAIRMENT

Hearing is one of the basic senses that allow people to understand, adjust, learn from, and respond to their environment. For example, a person driving responds to the sound of an ambulance siren by pulling his car over to the side of the road. People judge the distance of a train by sound.

Hearing also provides people with a way to compare sounds for speech. While the lip movements used to say the words *bear* and *pear* may appear very similar, the difference between the *p* and *b* sound in these two words tells the listener whether you are talking about a piece of fruit or an animal. Most importantly, hearing is a necessary part of speech. In order to acquire speech and language skills, we need a way to receive language, figure out what it means, and express it. Hearing provides us with the passage to do so. If any part of the passage becomes blocked or impeded in some way, the entire system through which we hear, process information, and express ourselves will likewise become impaired. The development of communication skills will be altered. The child who has such a problem is described as having a hearing impairment. He is said to be working from a sensory deficit in that a basic sense has been altered.

A child who has a hearing impairment may be affected in any of several ways. His hearing may be normal in one ear and not the other, or both ears may be affected. He may hear loud but not soft sounds. He may hear sounds, but they may be distorted.

Signs and symptoms of a hearing Impairment may be difficult to detect in an infant. Normal hearing follows a developmental progression. A very small infant may only widen his eyes or change his breathing in response to loud sounds. A slightly older baby will turn toward a sound. Eventually children learn to tell the difference between sounds (the phone and doorbell, your voice and other voices) and will respond differently to different sounds (he will smile for your voice, not for someone else's). Babies also experiment with making different sounds. Speech develops as a baby's ability to tell the difference between sounds becomes more sophisticated, and as he is able to connect sounds with certain objects, people, and behavioral responses, e.g., "cookie," "no."

Signs and symptoms of a hearing impairment in a young child would be the absence of or difficulty with any of these developmental steps. Older children may have difficulty following simple directions. They may turn the volume high on the TV before they appear to enjoy it. They may seem to hear better on some days then others.

The diagnosis of hearing impairment is usually made by an audiologist—a person certified and trained in assessing hearing. He is able to make a diagnosis that tells you if your child's hearing is within normal limits; if it is not, the audiologist can tell what type of hearing loss your child has (where the blockage or impedance is), and what degree of loss your child has (mild, moderate, severe). He can also recommend a treatment plan.

The assessment is usually done with special equipment in a sound-treated room. Parents of younger children may be invited to remain with them during the testing. A hearing test is in no way uncomfortable for the child. Tests performed vary depending on the age and abilities of the child. The amount of information received also varies according to the age and abilities of the child. However, no child is too young or disabled for a hearing test.

Because hearing deficits are so difficult to observe, any child with associated handicaps (cerebral palsy, Down's syndrome, etc.) should have a hearing test. This would especially pertain to those who are slow in developing speech and language.

If your child has a hearing loss, medical treatment can sometimes solve the problem. An ear, nose, and throat specialist (otolaryngologist) or a doctor who specializes in problems related to the ear (otologist) should be consulted for treatment. Some types of hearing loss may be helped through the use of a hearing aid. If an aid is recommended, the audiologist who completes the testing will suggest one that is best suited for your child.

Your child's education will also be a part of his treatment. The approach to his education will depend on the type and severity of his impairment, whether or not he has other handicapping conditions, and the method of teaching that is preferred by the teacher or school system with which he is involved. Whatever the educational setting and approach, it should enable your hearing-impaired child to participate as fully as possible, both educationally and socially.

VISUAL IMPAIRMENT

Vision, like hearing, is one of the basic senses that allows people to understand, adjust, learn from, and respond to their environment. The child who is visually impaired is also said to be working from a sensory deficit. As the acquisition of speech and language is affected by a hearing impairment, so is the acquisition of other skills—such as cognitive and motor—affected by visual impairment.

The child who is visually impaired may be affected in any of several ways. One or both eyes may be affected. The child may see near and not far, or vice versa. He may have blurred, distorted, or double vision. Any one of many structures involved in forming and interpreting visual images may be damaged.

Normal vision, like hearing, follows a developmental progression. An infant will follow an object with his eyes. A slightly older baby will reach for an object he sees. Eventually children learn to tell the difference between people and objects they see (a ball, a cookie, your face and other faces) and will respond differently to different sights (smile at your face and not at someone else's, reach for a cookie and turn away from a vegetable). Babies also experiment with sight, playing peekaboo and looking for hidden objects. More difficult skills, such as stacking blocks, placing pegs in a pegboard, and matching colors, are learned as visual skills become more sophisticated.

Signs and symptoms of visual impairment in a young child would be the absence of or difficulty with any of these developmental steps. Older children may have difficulty in any phase of schoolwork or with sports and games.

The diagnosis of visual impairment is made by an ophthalmologist, a medical doctor who specializes in diseases and defects of the eye. He is qualified to prescribe treatment and perform surgery. An optometrist is a specialist in vision who is also skilled in testing and can prescribe corrective lenses and treatment programs. There are many types of visual impairments, and your child's diagnosis will depend on the type of impairment he or she has. The impairment may involve damage to structures of the eye or structures of the brain that are involved in receiving and understanding visual images; the distance one is able to see; the span of the visual field to the left, right, or up and down. Acuity may be affected mildly, moderately, or severely, in which case one may be partially sighted or totally blind.

Treatment for visual impairment may include surgery, medication, patching, corrective lenses, or eye exercises, and is prescribed by the ophthalmologist or optometrist.

Education, as part of the visually impaired child's treatment, will depend on the type and severity of your child's impairment and whether or not he has other handicapping conditions.

ANOMALIES

The term *anomaly* refers to something different or deviating from the normal. With children we most often hear the term *congenital anomaly,* which means that the physical makeup of the child at birth was different from what is considered normal. The difference may be as minor as an extra or missing finger or toe, or as major as a missing limb. Some children have many physical differences which affect limbs, facial features, internal structures, and so on. These children are said to have *multiple congenital anomalies*.

There is no need to discuss the signs, symptoms, and diagnosis of anomalies, since the differences are obvious on observation and examination. It needs to be stated, however, that certain known medical conditions result in specific combinations of anomalies or physical differences. The conditions known to produce congenital anomalies are too numerous to mention. The diagnosis sometimes includes the term *syndrome*, which refers to a set of symptoms that occur together.

The treatment for congenital anomalies may involve many professionals, depending on the degree to which the child's function is limited and to which his physical appearance is affected. Your pediatrician may refer you to one or several specialists, such as an orthopedist (bone and muscle specialist), a prosthetist (a designer and fitter of artificial limbs and other structures), or a general or plastic surgeon for treatment. A special educator or therapist may also be involved in treatment where a child's anomaly interferes with normal function and independence. Your doctor or you may feel the need for some help from a psychologist, psychotherapist, or social worker to help you give your child a good self-image if his physical appearance is so noticeably different that it interferes with his social emotional growth.

PROGRESSIVE OR DEGENERATIVE CONDITIONS

Progressive or degenerative conditions are those that become worse as time goes on. Some conditions result in death, while others may progress to a certain point and then stabilize or stop progressing.

The signs and symptoms of a progressive or degenerative condition include the child's general health progressively failing over a prolonged period of time, and/or a progressive decrease in physical activity. If such symptoms are present, your child should be seen for a medical checkup.

Your pediatrician will do testing to determine the nature of the problem, and may refer you to specialists for a confirmation of a diagnosis and for treatment.

In the case of conditions that will stabilize as the child grows older, treatment would consist of all medication and therapies to alleviate discomfort and delay the degenerative process as much as possible until the condition is stabilized.

There is a great deal of controversy about the treatment of terminal illness, particularly in the case of the terminally ill child. Generally, the goals of therapy are to alleviate pain and discomfort, to delay the degenerative process in the hopes of prolonging life, and to maintain the best possible quality of life for the child.

The controversy arises when forms of therapy that are prescribed for the purpose of prolonging life cause pain and suffering for the child. If there is no assurance that such treatment will ultimately cure the condition or save the child's life, some feel that they would rather forego such treatment since it lessens the quality of the child's life. That is, many parents feel they would rather not add a few years to a child's life if they are only years of suffering. Others feel that every day they add to the child's life is one more day of hope that a cure for his condition will be found. Each family must decide along with medical professionals what course of treatment would be best in a particular case.

It has been our experience that most parents feel it advisable to continue the terminally ill child's education whenever possible in the school setting. Going to school gives the child the benefit of peer interaction and socialization. It also allows him to live each day to its fullest in the mainstream of life.

In addition to medical professionals and educators, it may be helpful for the child and family members to receive emotional support. Many churches, synagogues, and hospitals have groups for people who are dealing with terminal illness.

SUMMARY

The general information contained in this section will hopefully give you some insight into how children are categorized in educational and medical settings so that their needs can be met most appropriately. If you desire information about a specific diagnosis, we would refer you to books about particular handicapping conditions. Ask your librarians, teachers, or doctors which books are most current and which are written for parents. Many older books contain obsolete information, and books written for professionals may contain certain medical jargon which is difficult to understand.

We have found that parents generally believe that a good understanding of how a child is affected by a specific handicapping condition aids them in accepting his actual limitations, setting realistic goals, and helping him to grow in areas of strength and ability.

7. DISCIPLINE

Discipline is an area of parenting about which there has been much discussion in the past few decades. Psychologists, doctors, sociologists, social workers, and the like have extensively theorized about this subject. The dictionary lists several definitions for the word discipline: 1) training that develops self-control, 2) strict control to enforce obedience, 3) orderly conduct, 4) a system of rules, and 5) treatment that corrects or punishes. It is obvious that even the first two definitions of this word can be interpreted as conflicting.

It is far beyond our scope to come up with any pat answers or theories on this subject. As has been our style throughout, we hope to share the experiences and suggestions of other parents. We also hope to illustrate how some methods of handling discipline will be the same for a handicapped and nonhandicapped child, while other methods may need to be adapted for a handicapped child.

Some families with whom we have worked maintain a very strict atmosphere in their homes. Others are more permissive with their children. In some homes, shoes must be removed upon entering, a shirt must be worn at the dinner table, certain language is forbidden, and curfews are strictly enforced. In other homes children may walk on the couch, eat in their bathing suits, express themselves freely, and come and go as they please. There is a great deal of middle ground between these two extremes, which is where most of the families we see function. It would be important to determine just about where your family functions, which rules are important to you and which are not.

Adam is the three-year-old son of the M.'s. He is the youngest of five children. Once a week Adam and his mother attend a class with three other children and their mothers. All four children in the class are about the same age and all have Down's syndrome. The class is run by a developmental therapist who works with the children and their mothers to teach speech and language, encourage appropriate play skills, stimulate overall learning, and facilitate social emotional growth. During the class Adam refuses to follow any instructions given by the therapist. He physically resists and cries when demands are placed on him to pay attention or complete a task. When given snacks, he turns his glass of juice upside down and spits food at the therapist.

On several occasions the therapist removed him from the group, placing him in a chair and turning him toward the wall. This naturally induced more and louder crying. His mother, present throughout the sessions, did not interfere or voice any opinion to the therapist about Adam's behavior or the method in which it was being handled in the class. She did remark often that Adam was probably tired or not feeling well. About halfway through the year, Adam's attendance became very irregular. He began missing sessions more and more frequently. About three quarters into the year Adam and his mother dropped out of the class completely. As is routine in educational programs, Mr. and Mrs. M. were invited to an end-of-the-year staffing to discuss Adam's progress during the year and the educational goals for the upcoming year. Both parents attended, along with all five of the M. children. The reading and reviewing of reports took approximately forty-five minutes, during which time the four older children played independently outdoors and Adam busied himself quietly with toys in the room. Mr. and Mrs. M. listened attentively to the reports, which stated repeatedly that Adam's behavior interfered with the learning and socialization process. Goals for the upcoming year included structuring Adam's behavior more appropriately.

When the therapist concluded her report, Mr. M. began to talk. "I don't believe in forcing a child to do anything he's not ready to do. Until I can explain to a child why he can or cannot do something, I don't tell him 'no' unless life or limb is in danger. I don't think that's fair. Adam can't understand why he shouldn't do certain things, and until he can, we allow him to do them. Our furniture is a shambles and our walls are covered with crayon marks. All of our children climbed on the furniture and drew on the walls until I could explain to them that playgrounds were for climbing and paper was for drawing. When they understood, they stopped. They are all very happy and well-adjusted children. That is what I want, happy and well-adjusted children who respect but do not fear me."

Mr. M. felt very strongly and his wife agreed that the progress Adam had made over the past three years was patiently encouraged. At home they had never forced him to do anything. Whenever he was resistant to playing a game or doing a task, they stopped and tried again at a later date.

The therapist pointed out to them that Adam may never understand a logical explanation of more complicated dos and don'ts. The M.'s repeated that "unless life or limb was in danger," they would not force Adam to do or stop doing anything until he understood why. It was agreed that during the upcoming year Adam's mother would handle his behavior during these weekly sessions as she saw fit. If it was felt by the therapist and the other mothers that his behavior was interfering with the other children's learning, he would be removed from the class.

The meeting took over an hour, during which time the M.'s four other children, ages six through fourteen, played happily outdoors—no squabbling, no interruptions from them. They appeared well behaved and happy.

Who could question these parents' right to raise their children as they saw fit?

There are several points to be made from the example of the M.'s. First, they had very specific guidelines they used in determining what behavior was and was not acceptable to them. If a child did not understand the logic behind his actions, he was permitted to act as he pleased. If he understood his actions, or his actions endangered someone, limitations were set. Secondly, both parents totally agreed on how the children's behavior was to be handled. Third, they were consistent in their methods with all five of the children at all times.

It appears that regardless of the atmosphere you establish in your home—strict, permissive, or somewhere in between—these factors are extremely important in teaching your children what you consider to be appropriate behavior. Establishing specific guidelines or rules and enforcing them consistently are critical aspects of any discipline program.

You may find that having a handicapped child alters some of your ideas on discipline. You may begin to find yourself making exceptions for your special child.

The B.'s have a beautifully furnished home. Although their furniture is not new, it is in excellent condition. Their two older children have an area of the house in which they are allowed to play. The living room and dining room are off limits to them except for sitting quietly and behaving in an adult manner. Ronnie, a developmentally delayed child, is the youngest of the B. children.

At age two and a half Ronnie was still not walking. When he developed the ability to climb onto and off of furniture, the B.'s were so excited with his new skill that they allowed him to do it anyplace in the house including on the living room and dining room furniture. When he did walk, at age three, he was allowed to climb and walk anywhere he pleased. Mrs. B. said, "I don't care if he walks on tables so long as he walks."

It is natural to be so happy your child has achieved a skill for which you have been working and waiting that you overlook how he is using his new skill. Is he using it appropriately or inappropriately? Ronnie was using his new skills inappropriately. Perhaps the consequences are not quite as destructive in this case as they may be in others. A child who learns to throw and then throws his food is quite annoying, but no different from Ronnie, who walks on the living room furniture.

It is important that all your children have the same privileges and the same limitations. If expectations are clearly known by all children, they can easily separate what you consider right from wrong. When what is wrong for one child is right for another, all your children will remain confused.

Treating all of your children equally is also important in terms of developing your handicapped child's self-image, and will be discussed in this sense in a later chapter. For now, the point remains· Do not accept any behavior from your handicapped child that you would not accept from your other children unless that behavior is involuntary; e.g., drooling, excessive movement, poor bowel and bladder control.

Another issue many of our parents have discussed with us is

that of achieving cooperation and compliance from their children at home and in public.

James, age three and a half, has mild muscle weakness on the left side of his body (hemiparesis) resulting in a mild motor problem. His parents and preschool teacher think that other areas of development are age appropriate. He receives physical therapy for his left side and is in a preschool class three times a week.

After he had been at school for a short time, his teacher noted that James was beginning to act up. He would refuse to play with other children or cooperate in the activities of the classroom. James's teacher called his parents. Mr. and Mrs. D. agreed that they had noticed the same noncompliant attitude developing at home, but they were at a loss as to how to stop it.

The D.'s came into school and talked with James's teacher and the school psychologist. The psychologist asked the D.'s to participate in James's preschool class that morning. The D.'s readily agreed.

On that day, the teacher had decided to finger paint. The table was covered with paper, and trays of paint were set out. Each child was expected to put on a paint shirt and find a chair. As the other children began to do so, James wandered over to the bookcase, pulled down a book, and began to look at the pictures. Mrs. D. approached him and said softly, "Oh James, look, the other boys and girls all want to paint. It looks like such fun! Don't you want to paint now too?" "No," said James firmly. His mother looked worried and continued, "We could paint a pretty picture to put up on the refrigerator at home. Won't that be fun?" "No," was the same reply. "I'm going to go paint, James," she finally said. She stood up, put on a paint smock, and began to paint. James continued to look at his book, but would look up and watch his mother every few seconds. After a short time, seeing James look, his mother said, "Come and paint, James, this is such fun." Again the reply was "No!" and James continued to read his book. This time Mrs. D. became angry. She walked over to James and said, "You are being a very bad boy. You come and paint right now or we'll go home." "No," was James's final reply.

Because there was quite a bit of the school day remaining, James's parents stayed and did not go home. As the day progressed, James did do some activities with the class. At such times his parents played with him, were happy, and said nothing. There were, however, a few more times that James decided not to join the group. At these *times his mother or father would approach him, cajole him, and coax him to join. Each time James flatly refused.*

By the end of the day Mr. and Mrs. D. were exasperated. They met again with the psychologist and teacher. They agreed that this type of behavior was quickly becoming quite typical at home and in public but they had no idea of what to do.

The psychologist began to talk. "The way you responded to James's behavior was by paying more attention to him when he was uncooperative than you did when he was cooperative. Before you disagree, let's look at what happened. When James didn't want to play, you immediately went over to him and tried to get him to play. This actually gave him attention for what was uncooperative or negative behavior. When you went over to paint without him, I think you were on the right track—you began to ignore his uncooperativeness. Remember what happened? He started to get interested and looked up from the book at what you were doing. You then asked him if he wanted to come over, but what you should have done was continue to ignore him. Later in the morning, when James was playing nicely, you seemed very happy, but you forgot to tell James how nicely he was playing. By not telling him, you did not pay attention to or reinforce his cooperative behavior.

After several sessions and some trial and error on the D.'s part, they began to understand what the psychologist was saying.

Sometimes, as in the case of the D.'s, it is very difficult to separate which behaviors to pay attention to and which ones to ignore. Many of our parents have needed someone else—a psychologist, teacher, therapist, or another parent—to point out to them how and when to take this approach in disciplining. For many children, the approach of ignoring negative behavior and reinforcing positive behavior works exceedingly well in achieving compliance and cooperation.

In developing realistic expectations of your handicapped child, it may be necessary to make some adaptations in the environment, or to do some special training. Examples are as follows:

Eric is a six-year-old child who can only move about his home by crawling. His parents built a toy box with very low sides. Eric is expected to put away his toys.

Joan is a twelve-year-old blind child. Her parents taught her the location of everything in her room and how to make her bed. Joan is expected to make her bed daily and dust and vacuum her room weekly, as are her brothers and sisters.

By making these adaptions in their homes, the parents of Eric and Joan are able to expect certain behaviors from their handicapped child. These behaviors are certainly realistic and comparable to the types of behavior they expect from their other children.

There are some areas of discipline in which your handicapped child may appear to be the exception; however, he need not be if they are handled discreetly. An example would be the issue of giving him some kind of special help that he needs at home. He may need to do exercises, learn to use special equipment, practice specific skills, and so forth. Many children we have seen resist taking time to do such work when, while they are working, brothers and sisters are out playing. Brothers and sisters asked to help with the special care of a handicapped sibling may resent doing so when their friends are outside playing. Forcing a child to study, exercise, or help in the routine of the household usually does not work. Parents have related to us that cooperation in such matters has been gained by taking the emphasis off specific chores and placing major emphasis on the responsibility.

A distinction must first be made between what things are done in your family out of necessity and what things can be left to choice. Cleaning, laundry, earning a living, mowing the lawn, making meals, and giving special help to a handicapped child all fall into the category of necessities. Such things as baking cookies, going on a picnic, watching TV, and redecorating your room are left to choice. Children need to know that by cooperating in doing what is necessary, they derive the benefit of the whole family having more time for choice activities.

Children need also to be aware that they each have special needs which are met by the family working together. One child may require a great deal of chauffeuring to friends' homes; another may need to be taken to dance or music lessons; another may need extra help in math or reading. Whatever the case may be, it is obvious—if examined carefully in every family—that each person's needs are met with help from other family members. The needs of your handicapped child should be met in the same way.

Developing the attitude in all your children that certain things are necessary and that the family works together for the benefit of all its members should alleviate resistance and resentment.

While suggestions about consistency and cooperation are meant to deter behaviors that require discipline, we are well aware that children do not always follow the path that even the most dutiful and conscientious parents set out for them. To put it simply, there are times when all children are just plain rebellious. What do you do when this happens? Do you punish your handicapped child as you do your other children?

Todd is a seven-year-old child of the O.'s. He is a twin. He has a physical handicap and his brother Ben does not. When Ben talks back to his mother, has a tantrum, or is disobedient, his parents spank him. When Todd talks back, has a tantrum, or is disobedient, his parents put him on the floor in a large closet. They partially close the door and leave him there for fifteen minutes.

When we first were told of this method of punishing Todd we were appalled. We reserved our judgment, but could not help asking why he was punished differently than Ben. The O.'s response was, "We wouldn't think of spanking a handicapped child." It turned out that Todd was totally aware of why he was not spanked, and he accepted being put in the closet as a rather common and logical punishment for his behavior.

It has been found that when parents exercise good judgment about when punishment is called for and when it is not, it does not matter if the routine punishment is spanking, removal to a designated room, or denial of privileges. The message that gets across to the child is the same. It has been theorized that children who are never disciplined feel unloved. In the case of the O.'s, their handicapped child was punished as was his brother when he misbehaved. The only difference was that the O.'s felt it was necessary to change the type of punishment from one child to another. In many households not only are punishments altered from child to child, but also dependent upon the actions and the age of the child. These are decisions parents must make in a manner with which they will feel comfortable and in which they will be able to maintain consistency.

There are times with all children when they are not at fault but you become annoyed with them anyway.

Karen, the fourteen-year-old daughter of the C.'s, has great difficulty swallowing her food.

On a particular day Mrs. C. had many errands to run. Karen's feeding was taking exceptionally long. Mrs. C. began to holler at Karen. She became so angry that she stopped feeding her, left her in her chair, and went outside to calm down. Karen began to cry, which made Mrs. C. even angrier. She had to get nourishment into Karen; she had to run her errands. She felt pressured and annoyed. On top of that, she felt guilty for being impatient with Karen. Angry and upset, she finished the feeding. Mrs. C. knew she was being irrational but she could not seem to control her anger at the moment.

Before you feel too guilty about losing patience with a child for something that is obviously not his fault, remember that discipline is usually handled in one of two moods. There are the times when you are calm and collected, and after carefully examining the situation you determine what you consider to be a logical and appropriate consequence. The primary message a child receives when discipline is handled in this way is, "I have to pay a price for behaving inappropriately." There are other times when you are so upset that you are shouting whatever angry words pop into your mind. The primary message a child receives when parents are shouting is, "My parents really feel angry." The secondary message they may get is, "I did something that made them feel angry." If the child did nothing, however, he may only be left with the first message and not take any blame on himself.

When you are very angry about something a child does, the actual discipline or consequence for his actions is best decided after you have calmed down. Spanking when you are angry may do more physical harm than you intend. Punishments made up in anger are not likely to be followed through.

In a case such as Karen's, where she did nothing to elicit Mrs. C.'s anger, it is important that the parent let her know that she is not responsible. It is sometimes difficult to think logically when you are angry. There is a tactic, however, that can be used, and if you can develop the habit of using it in situations such as these, your child and you will probably feel better. The trick is, avoid the word *you* and use the word *I*. "I feel so rushed" comes across very differently than "You take so long to eat." A second tactic and probably a very honest one is an apology for taking out your own anger on your child.

A final point to be made in discussing the example of Karen is this: Most families, because there is more intimacy between them than with friends, take out frustrations and anger on each other at some time or another. You have a bad day at work; you come home and holler at your spouse because it seems safer than hollering at your boss. Someone at school bullies your child; he comes home and bullies his little brother. These are fairly common occurrences in families. If you do indeed accept your handicapped child as a total person and worthwhile family member, do not protect him from human experiences. Trust him as you trust other family members to handle these experiences. Do not waste precious time feeling guilty. Accept your human imperfections and trust your child to accept them.

A common trap parents fall into with handicapped children more than nonhandicapped children is game playing centered around issues of dependence.

Helen is a blind child, age ten. All of her clothing in her closets and drawers is arranged so she can distinguish one item from another as well as the colors of items. Her parents have taught her how to find exactly what she wants to wear. Each morning her parents awaken her in plenty of time to get ready for school. Every few minutes one of them reminds her to hurry and get dressed. Fifteen minutes before the school bus is to arrive, Helen is still sitting on her bed in her socks and underwear. Routinely, one of her parents ends up going to her room and assisting her in the remainder of her dressing.

Helen's teacher has reported to her parents that at school Helen finds everything she needs with no problem, and after swimming class Helen dresses herself completely in ten minutes.

Helen is obviously playing a game at home. She is able to find her clothes and dress herself, but prefers to remain dependent on her parents. Such a behavioral pattern may evolve out of a real need of parents to save time, but ultimately develops into a time-consuming game.

It is important at times to get things done as quickly as possible. It is almost impossible to consistently give a handicapped child sufficient time to do something that is difficult for him. One must, however, be cautious to avoid habitually taking over when a child can in fact do something on his own. When it does become necessary to assist, the trick of using *I* instead of *you* would also be appropriate to use. "I know you could dress yourself very well if I gave you a little more time. I'm just so rushed right now, we'll do it together," sounds very different from, "You take so long to dress, you'd better let me dress you today because you have to hurry." As a rule, enough time should be allowed for a child to take care of his routine daily activities independently if he is able.

Should you already be trapped in overinvolvement and want to free yourself, the process will take some time. You might start by setting up situations in which you can realistically impose a consequence if the child refuses to assume independence.

Mrs. R. announced at dinner that she would have a special dessert before bedtime. Everyone who was downstairs, bathed, and in pajamas by eight o'clock could have some dessert. At six-thirty she reminded everyone about the treat, giving Diane, her handicapped daughter, plenty of time to get ready. Between six-thirty and seven, Diane called to her several times to ask her help with different things: "Help me wash." "Help me dry." "Help me get my top on." Each time Mrs. R. pleasantly replied, "Sorry, I'm busy. You can do it yourself." Diane wasn't used to such answers, and by seven-forty-five her calling became nagging and whining. Mrs. R. remained pleasant and reassuring. When at eight o'clock Diane still was not ready for bed, Mrs. R. went upstairs and said, "Gee, I'm sorry, Diane. We're all ready for our dessert now. You will need the extra time to finish getting ready for bed. Put your pajamas on and go to sleep." "I can't," replied Diane. "I know you can do it just fine, but if you don't want to, go to sleep as you are."

The situation Mrs. R. set up was harmless, and she was able to get her point across. A child who cannot be left alone could not be told, "Hurry or we'll leave for the picnic without you." You would never follow through and the point would be lost. This is why situations often need to be set up rather than attempting to break the dependence pattern in normal everyday tasks. It is not likely in such tasks that you would be able to carry out your threats.

It is also important to be aware of a child's actual limitations and his abilities, as well as the time he needs to accomplish a particular task. If these things are not known, your expectations may be unrealistic and your child and you may become frustrated. As mentioned, breaking an established pattern is a long process. The sooner a child is using his maximum ability, however, the less time you will need to spend attending to his daily needs and the more time you can spend together enjoying each other.

Parents of severely handicapped children often are confused about whether or not there is a need for discipline. During a routine evaluation one mother was asked, "Does your child understand the meaning of the word *no?*" The mother replied, "I don't know. I've never had any reason to say no to him." Severely handicapped children often have a way of saying no. Since they do, it should be acknowledged, and they should also be helped to understand what it means when others indicate no to them. Their way of saying no may be obvious, such as noise or physical resistance; it may be subtle, such as removing eye contact or turning their heads away.

The importance of understanding the word *no* is in giving the child the ability to appropriately exercise control over his environment, and for a parent to exercise control over a child if this is necessary. An example of how a severely handicapped child may be helped to develop the concept of *no* in an appropriate way would be as follows:

Kim has a severe mental and physical handicap.

At meals, Kim would spit out certain foods. As Mrs. H. attempted through trial and error to figure out what the foods she spit out had in common, or when during the meal she began spitting, she realized that if she gave Kim a drink after she spit, she resumed eating.

Kim's teacher suggested that Kim's mother begin giving Kim choices. After several bites, Mrs. H. would hold up the food on one side and ask Kim, "Do you want more to eat?" If Kim did not look at the food, Mrs. H. said in a stern voice, "No, you don't want more to eat now." She would then hold up her drink on the other side and ask, "Do you want a drink?" If Kim looked at the drink, she gave it to her, saying pleasantly, "You want a drink." Kim eventually learned to make choices with her eyes, and to have some idea about what no means. It is possible that she was only tuned in to the pleasure and displeasure in the tone of her mother's voice; however, it established a way for Kim to exercise some control over her environment in an appropriate manner, and for her mother to establish a method of discouraging inappropriate spitting behavior.

Something that often concerns parents is having to decide whether annoyances and tantrums are strictly behavioral or if a child in fact is not feeling well. In the case of children who cannot talk, this is particularly disturbing, especially if no obvious symptoms of illness are present and you are wondering if your child is in pain or discomfort. The child who is carrying on, waking during the night, and cannot be soothed should have a medical checkup before discipline is enforced for annoying behavior.

In a previous chapter we briefly mentioned that siblings, relatives, and friends may pamper, spoil, or overindulge a handicapped child. If you disapprove, we suggested that you try to discourage this with an honest approach. Explain your methods of discipline to people who have extensive involvement with your child and emphasize the importance of everyone's being consistent for your child's benefit.

Do not get overly concerned if, after you have tried, a particular person continues to make exceptions for your child. Children quickly learn who will tolerate certain behaviors and who will not. Parents often wonder why some children behave one way in school and another way at home. The answer is that certain behaviors tolerated at home are not tolerated at school, and certain demands that are placed on children in school are not placed on them at home.

Your child's behavior with you will depend on your limits and expectations. His behavior with others will depend on their limits and expectations. Unless you feel someone is doing harm to your child, accept his relationships with others for what they are.

SUMMARY

In this section we have discussed those ideas on the subject of discipline that have come up most often in our conversations with parents, teachers, psychologists, social workers, and therapists: 1) Realistic limitations and expectations for your children should fit your own value system. 2) The limitations and expectations set up should be the same for your handicapped and nonhandicapped children insofar as possible. 3) Ignoring negative behavior and reinforcing positive behavior is an effective way to discipline children. 4) Provide the physical environment and special training that will allow your handicapped child as much independence and responsibility as possible. 5) Cooperation is best gained when children understand how they contribute toward meeting the needs of the total family. 6) A child who is continually disruptive for no apparent reason should be medically checked. 7) Help your children to understand when anger is and is not directed at them personally. 8)

Seek to develop an adapted communication system with a severely handicapped child so that his behavior is manageable. 9) If you cannot control others' relationships with your children, accept them as they are within reasonable limits.

Discipline, as we have discussed it, is an ongoing process. It would be difficult to feel totally prepared to handle every situation that arises where a decision needs to be made regarding a method of discipline. Sometimes hasty decisions are made and reconsidered. Sometimes the most thoughtful plan does not achieve the results you wanted. Our suggestions and examples can hopefully give you some further direction in establishing guidelines for discipline in your home.

As a member of your family, your handicapped child shares equally in the discipline process. He, like all other children, will look to you as an example and an enforcer of the moral and social standards you have established in your home. To make necessary exceptions for your handicapped child would show an understanding of his limitations. To make unnecessary exceptions for him would be to deny him whatever moral and social growth he is capable of achieving.

8. SOCIALIZATION

SOCIALIZATION WITHIN THE FAMILY UNIT

Children learn social skills from their environment. They learn what is acceptable behavior and what is unacceptable behavior. They learn to control their behavior in public places. They learn what is appropriate and when it is appropriate. Children learn such behaviors by the example and discipline of their parents and teachers. They also learn such behaviors through peer interaction.

Social skills are taught to normal children in many ways. They learn by the example set for them by parents, siblings, and peers. They learn from the discipline that governs their lives. They learn from the verbal reminders ("Wash your hands," "Don't talk while you're eating") that parents provide. These skills, likewise, must be taught to the handicapped child.

The social and emotional growth of children is extremely important. In order to establish motivation and to encourage growth in learning, the child needs a strong basis for social and emotional development. This basis needs to be established first in the home. Many activities that occur naturally in every family setting help a child to develop social skills.

Sarah is five years old. She has cerebral palsy and has much difficulty eating. She is still unable to feed herself, and when fed, the process requires at least forty-five minutes. Sarah is fed separately before the family sits down. Then, at dinner time, she joins the family with a toy to occupy herself with while they eat. Sarah's mother and father feel that although they must feed Sarah separately, she need not feel isolated from the family fun. They also feel that when Sarah is able to eat dinner with them, she will better understand how to behave during mealtimes.

Sarah's parents have indeed recognized the need for Sarah to socialize appropriately within the family. When they discovered it was impossible to feed her during their own mealtime, they adapted their life-style slightly to provide Sarah with the interaction she needs within the family.

Mealtime, for many families, is a time of sharing. They share the daily events, they share funny memories, they share each other. It is not a time to exclude a child simply because he does not yet possess the skills needed to participate independently. Nor is it a time to burden yourself with a child who demands your full attention for feeding. Sarah's parents have found, for them, an excellent way to allow for socialization while preserving a true sense of family unity.

Bill is eight years old. He was born with a visual impairment. Bill's sight is so limited that he is unable to enjoy television. When the family is watching television, Bill knows that he cannot ask questions during a program, but must wait until a commercial to interrupt others' viewing. He occasionally brings something else into the family room so that he is occupied while the family is watching TV. If his parents feel that a program is of particular interest to him, they explain the program beforehand. Bill knows that he is always welcome to watch television with the family.

Bill's parents want him to learn how to socialize within the family appropriately. They know that it is not appropriate to bother others with questions during a television program. They know it is inappropriate to listen to a radio or stereo while the television is on. They want to teach Bill what is acceptable and unacceptable behavior when others are watching television. If they are successful in doing so, they will be making it easier for Bill to socialize with others.

Bill's and Sarah's parents have demonstrated how to make minor adaptations for a handicapped child, but more importantly, they have demonstrated that there are many more times that a handicapped child will have to adapt to his environment.

The adaptation that Sarah's parents made was to feed Sarah before the family's dinner time. The adaptation that her parents required of her was that she join the family during dinner and learn to behave appropriately during mealtimes.

Bill's family also made adaptations for him. They would explain special programs to him beforehand or during commercials. They encouraged his questions at appropriate times. Bill was then forced to made adjustments of his own. He learned to listen carefully, to wait with his questions, and to find something else to occupy himself with if he lost interest in the television program.

It is likely that regardless of your child's handicapping condition or the severity of it, *he* will be the one ultimately responsible for adjusting to his environment as best he can. By teaching your child what others will expect from him, you are providing for him a greater likelihood of success in social situations. Not only will his family, his peers, and his relatives make adaptations for him, he too must recognize the need to adjust to his environment.

Many parents have expressed conflicting ideas about how to increase socialization within the family between siblings. Some parents feel that the "burden" of socializing with a handicapped sibling should not be placed upon any child. Others feel that handicapped or not, every child should play with his siblings. Many times the answer to this conflict lies within your own children and their individual differences.

Jody has a weakness in both of her arms. She cannot throw a ball well, nor can she catch one. Her older brothers often play together on a neighborhood baseball team. Even if chosen to be captains for the day, neither of them likes to choose Jody to be on his team. When Jody's mother found out about the way Jody's brothers were treating their sister, she was furious. She demanded that from that point on they always choose their sister first. While the boys did as they were told, they made it known to Jody that they did not want to do so. After a short time, Jody stopped playing ball with her brothers. She also stopped playing with them during other activities.

Many times children will find ways to work out difficult situations for themselves. They learn how to play effectively together by learning to respect one another. They do not learn how to accept others and to understand one another's differences by being forced to do so. Jody's mother had many other alternatives open to her. It is obvious that the one she chose, that of forcing, did not work.

There are times when simply listening to your children will enlighten you as to why they do not wish to play with a sibling. A child's reasons may range from less valid ones—"She's too much of a pest!"—to more valid ones—"She does not understand the game!" In talking with them, you may begin to understand what is causing the tension between siblings, and can determine if parental intervention is indeed necessary.

Another alternative may be to watch inconspicuously as your children play. Are they learning to be tolerant of each other's differences? Is the behavior you see typical of the way your child plays with other children? Is your handicapped child demanding more attention than normal? Can your handicapped child truly participate in all the free play of your other children? By watching and answering questions similar to these, you may be able to determine the causes of the friction between your children and begin to help them to correct it.

Let us now take a look at another example of how siblings learned to socialize.

David has visual perceptual problems, and therefore cannot judge distances or depths well. He has a great deal of difficulty in many sports because of this. David admires his older brother, Todd, and follows him everywhere he goes. Todd was embarrassed when David did so poorly playing ball or any other sport. Because of this, he tried to avoid being followed by David. Their parents anxiously watched as this took place, and finally Mrs. P. asked Todd if David could just be a batboy one day. On another day she asked Todd if David could help "coach." On another she asked if David could just watch him play. Eventually Todd began to find many things for David to do which did not require much skill. David and Todd continued to play together often.

Todd and David solved their conflict quite nicely with only minor interference from their parents. They needed only to be guided in the right direction. Once they were offered alternatives to their problem, they were able to create new solutions.

Not all conflicts between siblings work themselves out so nicely. Sometimes it requires trial and error on your part. Sometimes there is no "good" solution. Many times there are events in which it would not be appropriate for a handicapped child to socialize with his siblings.

For example, if an older sibling had a date on a weekend night and a younger child wanted to go too, it would be inappropriate to allow this. Another example may be if a younger brother wanted to be with a sister and her girl friends too often. This also may be unhealthy to encourage. In both these examples it would not be wise to encourage these interactions, not only for the sake of your handicapped child, but also for the sake of his nonhandicapped sibling. The point to be made is that your children can appropriately socialize with one another in some situations, but there may be many events in which it would not be appropriate for siblings to socialize.

There may also be events in which it would be good to encourage social interaction, after certain adaptations have been made. If a child wanted to go with his brothers or sisters to a beach for the day, without his parents, but his siblings were unable to maneuver his wheelchair in the sandy areas, it may be suggested that a wagon be used in place of the regular wheelchair for the day. Another example may be siblings who wanted to shop together for a parents' anniversary surprise, but recognized that the handicapped child could not yet take public transportation. An adaptation may be for one parent to drive them to the shopping center or store, leave them alone while they shop, and return to pick them up from the store. These simple social events may add a whole dimension to your child's life that he finds very necessary. Look for alternatives for him in order that he may experience such interactions with his siblings.

Many parents have related to us that although they recognize strong social desires on the part of their handicapped children, they see their children as realistically incapable of fulfilling such desires. For example, an eighteen-year-old boy, diagnosed as having Down's syndrome, told his parents repeatedly that he had a girl friend and wanted to take her out Saturday night in the family car. While his parents felt he had enough social desire to date a girl, they questioned his ability to fully understand dating and all that it entailed. They also recognized that without the reading and judg-ment skills necessary to drive a car, their son would probably never be able to obtain his license.

Another example is of a physically handicapped fifteen-year-old girl. In her desire to "be more like her friends," she discontinued taking necessary medication and had to be hospitalized for a lengthy period of time. Her parents did not want to constantly point out her handicap to her; however, they felt it was necessary for her to understand what made her different from her friends and why she must continue her medications.

Many children, handicapped or not, have social desires that exceed the level they are capable of handling: a sixteen-year-old who wants to drink liquor, a fourteen-year-old who wants a job after school, a seventeen-year-old who wants to marry, for example. To some extent, this social discrepancy may appear larger in the handicapped child. Although they understand the face value of identifying with peers, driving, and dating, these children may not be able to physically or mentally respond to the subtleties within those social desires.

The best approach to take in these situations is to explain to the child exactly what is needed. For example, he needs to read in order to pass a driving test; he needs medications in order not to be sick, he needs money in order to take out a date. Children may respond to these explanations by appropriately trying to rectify their situations; this is fine. Children may alter some of their expectations based on these explanations; this too is fine.

It is important to remember that a child's first exposure to social interactions begins in the home. It is necessary to use these first events to begin demonstrating good behavior. It is important that you, as a parent, show your handicapped child how to make adjustments on his own in order that he may benefit from much-needed social interactions. It is necessary that you show him how to respond naturally to people he will encounter.

This growing experience need not be for the sole benefit of your handicapped child. All children need to learn the differences and similarities in people and how to respond to them. While it is healthy for your handicapped child to share in the excitement of their brother's or sister's Little League game, band concert, or school play, it is also healthy for your other children to share in the special events of your handicapped child. These special events may be in the form of local Special Olympic Games or school functions.

Some families we know took a unique approach to increasing the understanding of a sibling's handicap by "creating" handicaps in the other children. The sister of a blind child wore a mask covering her eyes and tried to go through her whole day that way. Another sibling confined himself to a wheelchair for the day, while still another sibling tied one of his hands behind his back for the day.

At the end of the day the families sat down to talk about their experiences. The parents guided the discussions so that no one left feeling sorry for their brother or sister, but rather they left with a better understanding of the problems their brothers and sisters experience.

By providing your family with experiences such as these, you are increasing the awareness of the entire family to the similarities and differences within one another. By sharing and participating in each other's lives, making necessary adjustments for one another, and continuing to act in a cohesive manner, your family may enjoy some of the richness that is provided by having a handicapped child as a member of the family.

SOCIALIZATION OUTSIDE THE FAMILY UNIT

A common concern among parents is how their child will participate in peer groups. There are many reasons why parents find it difficult to find appropriate peer groups. Some families live in rural areas where the likelihood of there being special centers and programs is lessened. Some families think that because of the type or severity of the handicap their child has, a peer group would be impossible to find. There are many parents who think that their handicapped child should not socialize with other handicapped children, but should be encouraged to socialize with nonhandicapped children, but often it is difficult to find groups willing to alter activities enough to include a handicapped child.

Peer interaction is essential for the child's overall emotional and social development. As a parent with a handicapped child, it may be necessary for you to give additional thought to *how* your child will experience this crucial step in development.

If your child is very young, there are many mom-and-tot or dad-and-tot groups offered through your local park district. These same kinds of groups can also be found through the YMCA and YWCA in your area. Religious organizations, county and township agencies, and community colleges are also becoming aware of these needs. Seek out such groups by contacting any of these social service agencies or public agencies.

Do not overlook the baby-sitting services offered by bowling alleys, church organizations, and colleges. These too provide excellent peer interaction with adult supervision. An additional benefit of these groups is that you too can relax and enjoy the company of your peers.

If your child is of school age, a great deal of peer interaction can be accomplished within the school system. For this reason it is good to know the children who are in your child's class at school. Is he in a self-contained class? Is he being mainstreamed? Is he no longer eligible for school services? If after looking at your child's peer interaction you feel that he is in need of more or different kinds of social situations, there are local and national agencies that may provide help for you.

Both the Boy Scouts and the Girl Scouts provide groups for the handicapped youngster and young adult. Depending upon the type and severity of handicap your child has, the Scouts will attempt to integrate your child into existing troops and modify the activities within the troop if that becomes necessary. In any case, they welcome all youngsters to the scouting world.

Many organizations dedicated to helping parents—such as the Association for Retarded Citizens, United Cerebral Palsy Associations, Inc., and the Association for Children with Learning Disabilities—also provide recreational and social groups for children. You can contact the agency most likely to have a suitable social group for your child by either using the phone book or talking with your child's teacher.

Many parents have related a common concern that as their child has grown and left the school system, much of his social contact is cut off. Parents have noted their child becoming withdrawn and lonely because they no longer see their friends from school on a regular basis.

Recently, parents have begun to band together and form social clubs so that such contact continues after a child's school years. They have found that with a little advertising they themselves can begin a social group for their children. They use local newspapers, religious or fraternal organizations to find members as well as to gain financial support.

Meetings take place in members' homes, churches, library meeting rooms, or various public meeting facilities. Oftentimes the club members have their own ideas about things they would like to do within their club. These things may include social functions, fund raisers, or educational outings.

It is important to realize that such social clubs need not limit themselves to sedentary social activities. For example, a group of young adults, all of whom have profound hearing losses, have formed a softball team. They drew up a roster and became a team within their local park district league. After three years of play, they are considered one of the toughest teams in the league.

Throughout your child's life there will be many social functions available outside the family. These may include such activities as common as shopping, going to a restaurant, movie, or bowling.

Playing sports is socializing. Going on outings such as to the beach or on a picnic—that too is socializing. Going to a church or synagogue is socializing—being anyplace with people is socializing. As we have stated earlier, by developing independence in public places, there will be more of these opportunities for your child to socialize.

Another fine opportunity for socialization can be found in summer camps. These camps may be day camps or residential camps. Some handicapped children may not be able to attend a regular camp, but many special camps are available. The best way to become informed about the camps your child would be interested in is to contact The Exceptional Parent Bookstore (Room 700, Statler Office Building, Boston, Massachusetts, 02116) and ask for a special theme reprint from *The Exceptional Parent* magazine. The reprint, entitled "Recreation and Leisure," will include a list of summer programs. Also, if you subscribe to the magazine, there are many advertisements describing various residential camps.

For the day camps in your area, contact your local school district and make them aware of your needs. They may be familiar with an existing program or be inclined to begin a new program. Once again, use your parents organization to obtain additional information about summer camps in your area.

Exposing your child to the types of groups we have mentioned will be rewarding. Given the opportunity and your gentle guidance, your child's own personality will grow and develop. As your child continues to gain experience, you will discover a facet of his personality that may only be recognized during peer interactions.

YOUR PARENTAL ROLE IN SOCIALIZATION

As a parent, you will need to provide your child with various social experiences and appropriate social skills. You must also work continuously to develop a good self-image in your child and to teach self-discipline to your child. Many times, developing a child's self-image will insure the confidence necessary for social interaction. Many times your disciplining will develop your child's social skills. It is important for you to recognize that your behavior toward your child will have a definite impact on his ability to function on a social basis.

If you find that your child cannot learn a behavior from example, teach it to him through discipline. For example, a parent continuously reminded her five-year-old son to flush the toilet, but was unsuccessful in establishing the routine with her son. Eventually, whenever her son left the bathroom without flushing, he was not allowed to play with his toys for five minutes. Whenever he remembered, his parents praised him. He eventually learned, through discipline, the appropriate social etiquette.

If you are successful in building and maintaining a good self-image for your child, his social skills are likely to benefit. Sometimes, however, you must take the lead in showing your child what is acceptable and what is not. You must be the one to initially discriminate between what is acceptable in public places and what must be done in the privacy of the home, bathroom, or bedroom.

Whenever possible, treat your child as you would any child his age. Do not allow him to interrupt when others are talking; do not allow inappropriate eating habits if he is capable of better skills; teach your child the social graces and manners he needs and make him practice and use them. In some ways you may find yourself being harder and demanding more socially of your handicapped child than you feel you may of any other child his age. This by itself may not be harmful. Sometimes handicapped children are unable to distinguish when it is OK to let manners slide a little bit. The importance lies in determining what is socially important for *your* child and finding ways to instill that behavior in your child.

Even though your child may be severely handicapped mentally, it may be socially important for him not to be dressed in public places, not to be considered an infant. It becomes socially important and worthwhile because it affects not only the way he feels about himself, but also the way you and others feel about him.

Aside from projecting a good self-image and self-discipline, you must allow (or force) yourself to recognize all of your child's abilities. Do not further handicap him because you cannot see all that he is capable of achieving.

Michael is a sixteen-year-old physically handicapped boy. Since Michael was an infant, he has never been left alone. His parents have found relatives and friends to stay with Michael whenever they have needed to leave him. Because of this, Michael's parents have severely restricted their social life, and continue to do so. Although Michael attends school within his local high school program, his parents have refused any transportation arrangements. They have repeatedly stated that they would feel better if they themselves drove Michael to school each day. In school Michael has learned basic homemaking skills, and needs little assistance to manage public transportation once the route has been laid out for him. At home

Michael is not allowed to take buses, cabs, etc., at any time. If it is necessary for him to shop, go to the barber or doctor's office, Michael's parents drive him. He is not allowed to travel independently about town or to function independently at home. Michael discussed this problem with his school counselor. When the counselor approached Michael's parents about it, Michael's mother replied, "I don't want him to experience failure. There's so much he needs me to help him with. I must always be there."

Aside from the fact that Michael's parents are not providing him with the privacy in social situations that most sixteen-year-olds crave, they are placing an additional stigma on Michael. That stigma is, "Michael needs his parents. Michael cannot be left alone. Michael is not independent. Michael is handicapped in more ways than just his physical limitations."

Overprotection and dominance are severely limiting to a child's ability to mature socially. Many parents, regardless of whether they have a handicapped child or not, must fight these feelings within themselves. In Michael's case they are restricting him from experiences and "normal" social interactions with his friends, independent of parental supervision. In Michael's life, this need not be the case.

Martha F. is an eighteen-year-old girl who has been diagnosed as having Down's syndrome. The F.'s continue to belong to a parents' group associated with Martha's school. In talking with other parents and Martha's teachers, they began to realize that they had not let Martha truly function as independently as she could. Martha had learned many housekeeping and independent living skills in school, and demonstrated these abilities to her teachers regularly. The F.'s found out from Martha's teacher and other parents that many students in Martha's class were left alone at home for several hours at a time, with no baby-sitter. Up until that time the F.'s had continued to arrange for sitters and to limit their social engagements. They recognized that because they had been so protective of Martha, they would need to change things gradually.

At first, Mrs. F. would go next door to a neighbor's for just a few minutes. Gradually, when she herself felt more secure, she would make quick trips to the supermarket, again leaving Martha alone. Soon Mrs. F.'s excursions became longer and longer and the distances greater. Currently, Mrs. and Mr. F. both work. Mr. F. arrives home two hours after Martha returns home from school. Martha is now able to be alone for that short time every day.

At the last parent meeting Mrs. F. remarked to a close friend, "I wish I had started sooner!"

As both Michael's and Martha's parents demonstrated, it is easy to fall into overprotective and domineering roles with a child. Michael's parents did not recognize the implications of their behavior. They failed to recognize how much more they were limiting themselves as well as their child. It is unfortunate that they may never see Michael function as independently as possible. It is unfortunate that because of their overprotectiveness they will also never see Michael develop all the social skills he is capable of developing.

SUMMARY

We began this section with a discussion about training—teaching the social skills that will help your child be accepted and enjoyed by others. We went on to talk about practice—providing experiences within and outside of the family where his skills are reinforced so he will learn to feel at ease in social situations. Training and practice will provide the basis for successful social interaction.

To review, we discussed socialization as it pertains to the family as a unit, to siblings and to peers. Your child's success in relating to others will be affected by the ability of others to understand and accept his handicap. A more crucial factor will be his ability to adapt to others. If your child has been taught to behave appropriately in social situations, it is likely that adaptions will occur naturally.

Your parental role as we have defined it involves enforcing social discipline, setting realistic boundaries, instilling confidence, and encouraging social independence. Beginning with the basics of training and practice, your parental guidance and support will provide the building blocks for healthy social interaction.

Your child's handicap will affect his ability to interact socially. His expressions of emotional attachment may be as simple as a smile and hug, or as complicated as entering into a marriage. Regardless of how your child is able to express his social awareness, it is important to recognize that the social aspects of his life will most likely be a major source of his happiness.

Socialization is a continuous process in your child's growth and development. As we prepare our children to live in an adult society, our goals are that they understand and be understood, enjoy and be enjoyed, and that they experience the love and acceptance that results from the formation of interpersonal relationships.

9. ALTERNATIVE LIVING ARRANGEMENTS

"SHOULD WE PLACE OUR CHILD IN A RESIDENTIAL FACILITY?"

As the parent of a child who is handicapped, you will be forced to make many decisions that other parents often take for granted. We have already discussed such concerns as medical, educational, employment, legal, and financial decisions. There is yet one more major decision which often needs to be made; that is, should we place our child in a residential home or school?

There are many questions you must ask yourself. Be prepared to answer frankly. The placement of a child outside of his home environment is an extremely emotional issue. For this reason, you may find disagreement between spouses, health professionals (doctors, therapists, etc.), educators, and family members. You may also find conflicting emotions within yourself.

It is important to recognize that this decision is one that many children make at a natural point in the process of maturation. The child who is eighteen years old and wishes to go away to school is an excellent example; the nine-year-old child who enjoys and looks forward to summer camp is another example. These children are acting as the decision makers of how, when, and where to leave home. So many times in raising a handicapped child this will not be so; instead, you as the parent will be the decision maker.

If your handicapped child is capable of participating in or autonomously making this decision, we strongly recommend that you encourage this. In such cases, the decision of where a child should live may be determined in a more natural context. Talk to your child and deal with his feelings regarding his home.

Another important factor to remember is that no decision should be considered irrevocable. If you decide to raise your child in the home, but are concerned that this arrangement may not work out, use the "trial period" method. Give yourself, your spouse, your child, and your family plenty of time to adjust, but recognize that simply because this was your first choice there is no need to consider it your last.

The same should be true of any residential setting you investigate. No decisions should be final until you determine them to be.

Another factor which is (thankfully) changing today is that residential placement need not mean institutionalization. Many of us can remember times when state and private institutions were crowded to unsanitary limits. These were times when handicapped children were merely "taken care of" and "put away." Within such institutions vocational and social skills were not encouraged. Numbers, not quality of care, were important. Such institutions encouraged uniformity, passivity, disparity, and inequities. They elicited pity, not understanding. They sought seclusion, not community interaction. They offered humiliation and shame, not pride, self-respect, and dignity. Indeed, they pursued goals that directly contrast the "normalization" that parents currently seek.

Normalization is a process by which those citizens who are handicapped are encouraged to lead lives as similar as possible to those citizens who are not handicapped. This idea has been extended to residential facilities. Normalization is fostered through the attitudes that facilities develop among the staff, the residents, the families of the residents, and the community in which they are located.

These attitudes are developed by such overt actions as establishing residential facilities within existing communities, encouraging residents to participate in community events, and providing work and recreational activities for residents. These attitudes are also developed by such covert actions as the treatment of residents as individual human beings, encouraging individuals to achieve their maximum potential, and developing awareness and acceptance within the community. In facilities such as these, residential placement does not mean institutionalization.

Should you place? The decision must be yours and, when possible, your child's. No one else knows your child better than you. No one else knows your family better than you. No one can tell you yes or no because they have had "more education about these things" or are "more objective regarding this decision." The decision will not be anyone else's to live with, and therefore no one's opinion is better than your own.

In many cases you will find people quick to take the decision out of your hands. Doctors, educators, professionals, friends, and relatives will attempt to provide you with their best advice. Try to remember our discussion about fact versus opinion. It is only their opinion that your child is better off at home, in a residential facility, or wherever. It is only their opinion that you or the members of your family will adjust better if placement takes place at birth, at the time of diagnosis, or at a later point in time. Such things are not yet known to be fact, therefore it is only *your* opinion that matters.

Coming to grips with your own and your family's feelings on placing your child may be a long and difficult process. Take the time to understand your feelings and those of your family. Also take the time to identify the facts about your home situation and alternative living arrangements. Below are questions that you and your family may want to consider after you ask yourself the question, "Should we place?"

EXAMINING THE FACTS

1. Are you physically able to care for your child at home?
2. Are responsibilities for the care of your child shared by family members, or does one person feel burdened with the major responsibility?
3. Do your child's special needs fit into a general life-style with which your family feels comfortable, or have you built a life-style around your child's needs in which family members feel limited?
4. Has there been disagreement among family members about whether your child can best be cared for at home or elsewhere?
5. Do you continue to have interests (social, educational, recreational, hobbies) apart from your child, or is all of your spare time devoted to his care?
6. Have you thoroughly investigated alternative living arrangements that would be suitable for your child?

7. Do you have time alone with your spouse, other children, and for yourself, or does the care of your child demand all your time?

8. Is your view of your child's abilities/disabilities similar to the views held by doctors, educators, and/or therapists who may have suggested placement?

9. Are you able to manage your child's behavior, or is he uncontrollably disruptive?

10. Are you able to provide educational, social, and recreational stimulation for your child in your present living arrangement?

11. Does your child seem bored with or left out of many of your family activities?

12. Does your child have critical medical problems about which you are always fearful or that you feel incapable of dealing with?

13. Has any change in your home situation (death, divorce, older children leaving home) altered the quality and quantity of care you are able to provide for a dependent child?

14. Do you see signs of maturation and independence that indicate to you that your child is capable of functioning on his own?

15. In the case of an older child, do you and your child frequently disagree about what his rights and privileges should be while living at home?

16. In the case of an older child, has your child talked about moving out?

17. What does your child benefit from while living at home? What about the home living arrangement impedes his total growth and independence?

18. What might your child benefit from in a "home" away from home that is appropriate for him? How would he be limited in such a "home"?

19. Can your child participate in this decision? What does he think?

EXAMINING FEELINGS

1. What have you been brought up to believe about homes for handicapped citizens? Are your preconceived ideas interfering with your decision?

2. What does separation mean to you in terms of you and your child?
   a) Giving him up.
   b) He does not need you any more.
   c) You are an inadequate parent.
   d) He would benefit from another living arrangement.
   e) Something other than the above statements.
3. Do you have fears about how others will care for and treat your child?
4. Do you worry about what family and friends will think if you place your child?
5. If you and your child were not living together would you feel:
   a) You should visit him daily because he may miss you.
   b) You should never visit him so he will forget you and adjust to his new home.
   c) You would visit him regularly, but help him adjust to living apart from you.
6. Do you find yourself frequently contemplating the decision of whether or not to place your child?
7. When you think about living apart from your child do you feel:
   a) Guilty.
   b) Relieved.
   c) Comfortable because it would be best.
   d) Uncomfortable because your home is the best place for him.
8. Do you visualize that living apart from your child would:
   a) Solve many problems in your family.
   b) Create many problems in your family.
   c) Not affect family problems one way or the other.
   d) Your family has no crucial problems so this question does not apply.
9. How do you visualize your future/your child's future:
   a) If your child lives with you?
   b) If your child lives apart from you?
10. Do you have concerns about how your child's growth and learning would be affected if he lives with other:
    a) Handicapped people?
    b) Nonhandicapped people?

If you take time to consider these questions and discuss them openly with your family, perhaps you can clarify and sort out many facts and feelings which will help you in the decision of "Should we place?"

Although you may be able to think through the issues quite rationally, it seems that the inner emotional struggle most parents experience in the decision-making process is unavoidable. We would like to share with you some of the insights we have gleaned from families who are considering placement, or whose children already live away from home.

Family unity does not seem to be altered when a child lives away from home. Once the initial adjustment period has passed, families regain and maintain the unity and intimacy that was established. Two examples come to mind as we reflect on this thought:

Heather and Randy are twins who were separated at six months of age. Both are handicapped; Heather mildly and Randy severely. It was evident soon after birth that Heather had mild delays and that Randy was severely affected by the period of respiratory distress that followed their birth. Mrs. and Mr. C., the twin's parents, had two other children. They decided that Randy's and their family's needs could best be met if Randy lived in a facility that could provide the medical care he continued to need, along with an educational and therapeutic program. They did not feel they could provide the best care at home with three other children, one of whom was also handicapped.

After investigating several homes, they found an appropriate facility. The family visited before Randy went to live there. Mr. and Mrs. C. explained the arrangement to the two older children.

Each weekend the family visits or Randy is brought home for a visit. As Heather began to understand that her twin brother did not live at home, Mr. and Mrs. C. explained as much as they could to her. Randy's name is always included in family discussions. Mr. and Mrs. C., as well as Heather and the two other siblings, call the facility where Randy lives several times during the week to talk briefly to Randy's caretakers and see how he is. Heather is now five years old. She talks about her brother Randy as frequently as she talks about her other siblings. If you ask, she will tell you that Randy needs very special care and lives in a special place where people who cannot eat regular food and play with regular toys get special food and toys just for them that they cannot get at home.

Curt moved away from home at age twenty-four. He was the only child left at home since his sister had married. His mother, prior to his moving out, had been totally involved in his care. Her social life had been very limited, as was Curt's.

Since Curt's graduation from school, he and his mother were together so much of the time that they seemed to find each other annoying on occasion. When Curt's father came home he frequently found his wife tired. Curt's sister and her husband did not enjoy visiting too much since Curt and his mother were frequently upset. After much deliberation and investigation of alternative living arrangements, Curt's parents found a "home" they felt would be suitable for Curt, and it was decided he would live away from his parents.

After Curt moved out, his mother became involved in the parent group where Curt lived. She found purpose as well as friendship in belonging. She had a way to be with Curt often, spend positive time with him, and socialize herself. Curt developed new relationships in his new "home." His father, mother, sister, and brother-in-law enjoyed visiting. They had more to talk about than they did when Curt was at home. Curt's parents' relationship improved. The whole family seemed happier and closer.

These two examples, one of separation at six months of age and one at twenty-four years of age, point out that the family unit can remain strong, perhaps be enhanced when an alternative living arrangement is viewed as a positive solution to a family's needs. The strength of the family unit can be considered unchanged when you ask yourself, "Should we place?"

Emotions can cloud facts. We have seen families who are considering alternative living arrangements so ridden with guilt and fear that they lose their objectivity. Some children who seem obviously ready to live independent of parents are held back by overprotective parents who find unrealistic reasons to keep them at home. Other children who are totally dependent and could benefit from the social atmosphere and stimulation that group living would offer are kept at home for reasons of guilt and fear. There may be good reasons to place or not to place a child. Guilt and fear, however, should not be the deciding factors. If you have these feelings, it is best to seek counseling and work through these feelings, and then reconsider the question, "Should we place?"

Several of the questions we provided for your consideration in making this decision revolved around dissension among family members. If dissension exists between you and your spouse or you and your other children pertaining to your handicapped child, we do not recommend that you make a decision because you feel it will provide the "cure" to the arguing. A child should not be a means of winning, losing, or settling arguments. There are likely to be underlying issues that have little or nothing to do with your child's handicap that are the cause of dissension in your family. Removing a child does not provide the cure for dissension. If there is frequent arguing in your home, we recommend counseling before making the decision, "Should we place?"

On occasion we have initiated a discussion with families about placement. In these instances we felt we were working with people for whom placement may have been a positive alternative, but who for one reason or another would not allow themselves to even consider the possibility. More times than not the question, "Have you ever considered an alternative living arrangement?" elicited a response such as, "No, I would never think of putting my child in a home." When pursuing the issue with these families we frequently discovered that they were influenced by family pressures, they had little or no idea as to what types of arrangements were available, or they viewed a separate living arrangement as "giving up" their child. If you review the questions we asked under the heading Examining the Facts, you may perceive that we believe that there are some situations in which at-home care may simply be inadequate.

Eric is the two-year-old son of Mrs. R. He has respiratory problems, a spinal cord lesion from which he is paralyzed from the waist down, and a tracheotomy which requires suctioning every few hours. He also requires tube feeding. There is only one parent living in the home, and therefore all of Eric's care falls on Mrs. R.

Eric is unable to cry, and because of this, his mother has no way of knowing when he is in distress except to observe his color. When Eric goes into respiratory distress, it is a life-threatening situation for which his mother must administer oxygen. The oxygen tank sits beside his bed at all times. His mother monitors him hourly throughout the night, as well as all day. She is in a relatively constant state of panic because of Eric's medical problems. She has one sister who lives nearby, visits frequently, and does errands for her, but feels inadequate when it comes to taking responsibility for Eric's care.

Eric's medical condition has been essentially the same for the past two years, with several emergencies arising for which he was hospitalized and then returned home. Mrs. R. receives welfare for personal expenses and medical care.

We felt in Eric's case that at-home care was inappropriate. His mother was at first resistive to discussing placement. As we discussed the facts of her situation, however, she acknowledged that it was the best possible alternative. Both Eric and his mother were disadvantaged by his living at home. Eric did not have the advantage of emergency medical attention at home if he needed anything more than oxygen. He could not be monitored twenty-four hours a day by a single person. His mother was becoming totally "disabled" in terms of her general health and her emotional stability.

Eric was finally placed in a skilled nursing care facility for which Eric's mother could receive financial assistance as a welfare recipient.

Under circumstances where at-home care may not be feasible, there may be an alternative living arrangement that would be more adequate. Although you may have strong feelings about keeping your child with you, different living arrangements may provide more comprehensive care.

We believe that answering the question, "Should we place?" often does not have a right or wrong answer. For this reason it is impossible to consider the issue in a pro/con dichotomy. The family and society are places where dynamic exchanges occur. You cannot successfully reduce this to a wrong versus right decision.

Remember that placing a child may be a natural progression in his development. It need not mean institutionalization, but rather a continuing part of life's experiences. Your decision (or the decision of your child) need not be irrevocable.

It is our hope that our questions and our statements have provided you with the food for thought that will lead to a comfortable conclusion when asking yourself the very personal and difficult question, "Should we place our child in a residential facility?"

WHEN TO PLACE

If your child's handicapping condition is such that it is recognizable at birth, the decision of when to place may be imminent. The birth of a child leaves many of us particularly vulnerable. Although it can be a happy experience, it can also be a physically and emotionally draining experience. Regardless of whether it is the birth of your first child or your fifth child, the experience is likely to leave you with some new feelings and some renewed feelings.

For many people, this time of their lives is an unstable period. You may have preconceived notions of birthing and parenting that you expect to fulfill. As we have already discussed, this time of adjustment and beginning to cope with the idea of a handicapped child can be very difficult. Although families may find themselves in a difficult and unstable period, some feel the need to make a decision soon after the birth of a child who has been identified as handicapped. We encourage you to review the points we have made earlier regarding placement; it is not a fixed irreversible decision, it is not a decision to be made by others, but rather by you and your family. Placing a child residentially may be good for some children and their families and not good for others.

Another period of time when the issue of placement occurs is when new or different needs of the family or child develop. A child's needs may include such things as increased medical attention or increased need for physical assistance. A family's need may arise from death or aging of the parents, instability or changes within the family structure. When such circumstances develop, it may be necessary to consider (or reconsider) placing a handicapped child in a residential facility outside the family unit.

Many times when a handicap is first identified, parents feel the need and desire to place but cannot find a suitable living arrangement. Other times educational or vocational opportunities appear to be brighter within the family's community, and living at home is a feasible arrangement. Then, at a later date, "better" or "more suitable" opportunities arise in environments outside of the home. In such cases the decision of when to place is answered when an appropriate living alternative presents itself.

There also comes a natural time period for investigating residential facilities—when a handicapped child becomes an adult. When exactly this occurs is uncertain and highly debatable, but it certainly does occur. As a parent it may be necessary for you to watch for signs of this development. Such signs may include increased independence and increased social or vocational needs. Although some children may never exhibit signs of independence, they are nevertheless considered adults at or around the age of twenty-one.

Recognizing your child as an adult may require a good deal of honesty on your part. Many parents find it difficult to objectively note subtle changes or advancements in their child's behavior. If you are unsure, talk to your child's teachers, supervisors, and therapists. Review the questions we have provided for you earlier in this chapter. Use all the resources available to you to determine if indeed your child's needs can no longer be met at home.

There are many families who must constantly reassess the living arrangements of their handicapped child. These families have children whose placement may change from hospital to home to hospital, or from hospital to residential care to home. Many of these children have medical problems in a constant state of flux. Some of these children may have emotional problems and may benefit from changes in placement as their behavior becomes stabilized. There can be many other reasons, however, for families to continuously evaluate the living arrangements of their handicapped child.

The problem of multiple placements typically puts additional strain on the family. In such cases we recommend that you coordinate your placements through one central agency. If your child is between the ages of three and twenty-one, your local school district can act as this agency. If your child is below three or above twenty-one years of age, you may consider seeking help from your local mental health department or department of social services.

Many parents have expressed to us that they were comforted by the fact that one social worker or representative knew their family circumstances. They found support and consistency in a single agency; however, many changes of programs were necessitated by their child's changing needs.

"When should you 'place' or change your child's living arrangement?" Our best answer/opinion is: If at all possible, wait until you are ready. Parents have expressed to us that they knew they were ready when 1) they knew their child's abilities and disabilities, 2) they knew their parental resources and limitations, 3) the family felt comfortable with the decision, and 4) the facts and opinions regarding a particular living arrangement were established. We have already discussed ways to determine your own, your child's, and your family's abilities and disabilities. Let us now look at how to feel confident about which living arrangement is best suited for your child.

WHERE TO PLACE

In seeking the best living arrangement for your child, it is recommended that you continuously review your alternatives. There currently exist various living arrangements for handicapped citizens aside from living at home. In some areas of the country facilities are growing and improving.

The current trends in living facilities for handicapped children and adults capitalize on providing quality supervised care. Many large institutions have reduced the number of residents and increased staff size. Smaller residential facilities are being located within established communities. Small group homes, halfway homes, and community living facilities are available in many areas. Emphasis is being placed on homelike facilities.

The concept of mainstreaming handicapped citizens into communities is also becoming more of a reality. Facilities that encourage community employment are likely to be in locations convenient to public transportation, work and recreational areas within the community. Contact with community groups is facilitated in such locations as opposed to the isolated "country" residential facility.

Another major trend is the greater emphasis placed on independence within the facility. This independence is being encouraged in adults, regardless of the type and severity of their condition. Today more homes and group living arrangements are available for citizens who at one time were thought to be too mentally or physically handicapped to function in a supervised facility. Limitations in social, personal, or financial independence were often cited as major reasons for rejection of an individual from many community or group homes. Frequently, the individual's only alternative to living in the family home was a large residential facility. Lately there has been a shift in emphasis to providing these individuals with smaller homes which foster greater individual freedom.

So much of what we have spoken of in this chapter is based on opinion and emotions. There is, however, much factual information that you should obtain about where your child will live. Recently many new options have developed with respect to living arrangements. The options which will be open to you will depend upon where you live, the space available in any given setting, and your child's abilities and disabilities.

The relationship of where you live and the facilities available to your child is not always clearly defined. In general, urban areas are likely to have more facilities to choose from than rural areas. States and communities with larger populations typically have more alternatives available. This is not to say that small, underpopulated areas are without services, or that those services are poorer or less advanced. It will be necessary for you to investigate the area in which you live to determine how many and what kinds of alternatives you have available.

It is not necessarily true that the "better" residential facilities are more difficult to get into than the "poorer" ones. Certain facilities are simply more crowded than others for any one of a number of reasons. Try not to be fooled by numbers or rumored reputations of any given facility.

Another factor that will influence your child's living arrangement is his individual abilities and disabilities. We are not saying that severely mentally, physically, or emotionally handicapped citizens should be refused placement in an appropriate residential facility. We are also not saying that such severe handicaps should, in and of themselves, force an individual into a living arrangement that does not challenge all the capabilities he does possess.

Being realistic about your child's abilities and disabilities does not preclude being idealistic about social, educational, and vocational opportunities presented to him. To be realistic about his limitations should not mean that you accept further limitations placed upon your child by others. Perhaps this thought will become clear in the following example.

Pam is a twenty-four-year-old woman. She has spent all of her educational years in special classes. Psychological reports indicate Pam is presenting skills (or functioning) in the trainable mentally handicapped range. At birth Pam was diagnosed as having Down's syndrome. Pam graduated from school three years ago at the age of twenty-one. At that time her teachers and parents agreed that Pam was very socially aware, but limited in her independent functioning. She was "limited" in that she could not handle money. Because of this she had difficulty shopping for food and clothes by herself. Pam also had difficulty in making decisions that required judgment skills. When the toilet overflowed she merely put the seat cover down and closed the bathroom door. When she blew a fuse at home she would merely walk out of the room, neglecting to tell anyone of the problem.

Such limitations caused Pam's mother to believe that the small residential supervised facility operating in the community would not be appropriate for Pam. She disliked the idea of sending Pam to the large facility run by the state, where little to no independent skills were encouraged. The community living facility, on the other hand, offered supervision coupled with the fostering of individual living skills in an apartmentlike setting. It worked on a system of levels in which the residents progressed at their own rate. The lowest level provided the greatest supervision, while the highest level offered almost no supervision.

After visiting the building and speaking with the counselors, it was decided that Pam would live at the home for a three-month trial period. Within three months Pam was calling her new apartment her "home." She visited her parents often, but spent few nights with them. There were many difficulties and problems encountered in those first few months, but Pam insisted on continuing to live in her own "home."

In Pam's case, what was needed was a place away from her parent's home to continue to develop her independent living skills. She needed her "apartment" to increase her self-esteem and self-confidence. She needed supervision for protection, guidance, and encouragement. By carefully weighing all the alternatives open to Pam and her family, they made their best decision as to where Pam should live.

We have taken a close look at how best to determine your child's abilities and disabilities and how they may be complemented by a living arrangement. Let us now look more closely at what living arrangements are available.

FACILITIES AVAILABLE

Residential Facilities

The main types of residential facilities available are state-owned and -operated, private nonprofit and for-profit facilities. Major differences between these types of facilities include their financial structure, their philosophy, and their population.

State-owned and -operated facilities have probably witnessed the greatest changes in the past few years. While the financial structure (money largely received from the government) has remained constant, the philosophy and the residential population have undergone noticable change.

Many facilities no longer consider themselves custodial operations. They look to develop their residents' social, educational, and vocational skills. The number of residents within individual facilities is likely to have experienced a decline, thus providing for a better staff-to-resident ratio.

State facilities unfortunately continue to be located far from many people's homes. They are likely to be located in rural areas where opportunities for employment are greatly reduced. Some continue to be understaffed or staffed with fewer professionals than may be found in smaller facilities.

Private nonprofit and for-profit facilities are also available in many areas. Such residential facilities, which tend to be smaller and established within the community, may be funded on a private or governmental basis. For this reason, the cost for such care varies. It should be noted that the quality of care provided is not directly related to how the facility is funded. Excellent programs exist under both financial arrangements.

Types of residential facilities vary greatly from state to state. We urge you to investigate your local programs before you search for living arrangements far from home. As we have previously stated, the current trend is to develop residential facilities within communities, near families, relatives, and friends.

Some of the advantages in these private facilities are that 1) facilities are located closer to your home—this may be because the number of private facilities is typically greater than the number of state facilities, 2) they may provide services only for a special type of handicapping condition (e.g., hearing impaired or visually impaired), 3) you may prefer an all-boy or all-girl living arrangement to the coeducational facilities typically offered by the state, 4) the number of residents may be smaller and it is likely that the staff-to-resident ratio in a private facility is better, and 5) they may be geared toward training specific vocational or educational skills.

The disadvantages may be that 1) your state institution may provide all of the above at lower or no cost to you, 2) although most private facilities are based on a sliding fee scale (the parents pay what they can afford), you may still be financially unable to place your child or adult in a private institution, and 3) good private institutions may not be available in your area.

Supervised Living Facilities

These are small group homes that operate with the goals of developing the individual living skills of each resident. Most of the facilities are developed in an apartmentlike atmosphere. Supervisors are provided and residents selected based on their individual abilities to function—to some extent—independently.

Most facilities are located within the community and attempt to integrate residents into community activities. The supervisors instruct residents in such activities of daily living as money management, cooking and housekeeping skills. Residents are continuously encouraged to develop greater independence in living skills so that 1) a resident will eventually live totally independent of the facility, or 2) the resident will continue to live within the facility, but at the greatest level of independence possible for him.

Supervised living facilities are referred to by many names: community living facilities (CLF), supervised living facilities (SLF), and adult training residences, among others. What makes them different from other residential facilities is their goal: to develop an individual's independent living skills to the greatest possible extent so that he or she may in the future be able to live independent of supervision.

In visiting and evaluating different residential facilities, it is important that you keep careful notes about the similarities and differences between them. The following is a list of considerations that you should familiarize yourself with before you make initial visits to various living arrangements. Some points may not apply to all facilities, but the list should provide you with an organized method of reviewing every place you visit.

Evaluating Residential Facilities
Physical considerations
1. Size
2. Population: type of handicapping conditions, ages
3. Ratio of staff to residents, day and night
4. Distance from home; availability of public transportation
5. Dietary considerations; independence at meals; choices for meals; eating facilities; sanitation
6. Overall cleanliness
7. Areas other than room or dormitory

Other considerations
1. Educational programs
2. Vocational programs
3. Recreational programs
4. Financial assistance
5. Community programs
6. Parent/family programs
7. Medical care/health services
8. Availability of counseling/advocacy
9. Staff: Ratio, attitude, training, turnover
10. Specific policies within the program

Foster Care

Foster-care facilities are sometimes available to families who need temporary but long separations from their children. It is assumed that in such cases the child will return to his home some time in the future. Foster care is usually provided within family homes. Once the child's immediate family is stabilized, the child then returns to his own home.

Foster care has been frowned upon by many parents and professionals. As it presently stands the system exhibits many problems. There are difficulties finding suitable foster-care homes as well as financial problems. There are many cases where it is likely the child will not be able to return home for a prolonged period of time— if ever. These children are sometimes shifted from one foster-care family to another with no end in sight.

Although problems do exist in the foster-care system, particularly as it pertains to the foster care of the handicapped child, for many children and families it is a necessary and vital system.

Respite Care

Respite-care facilities are becoming an excellent alternative for parents who need foster care or sitters, but for a much shorter period of time. Respite care provides parents with a period of temporary rest or relief in the caring for a handicapped child. Many parents in the past have received this temporary care from willing friends, neighbors, or relatives. Others have been less fortunate. Respite care offers parents a place to leave their handicapped child for short periods of time, such as overnight, or for longer periods of time—for several nights, usually up to two weeks.

Respite care apparently grew out of the need for emergency temporary care of handicapped individuals. Many times parents could not find qualified care for their children when emergency situations arose that required overnight or several nights of service. Presently many respite-care services are offered to parents who need temporary care for their children in nonemergency situations. Such times may include vacations or common social situations that demand a sitter.

There are several kinds of agencies that provide respite care but they can be broken down to primarily two kinds: 1) an agency that provides respite care within an existing setting, or 2) an agency that coordinates services of respite caretakers in their own homes.

An agency that provides services may do so in one of two ways: 1) They provide services in a residential facility set up solely for the purpose of offering respite-care services, or 2) they provide services within an existing facility where there are also other types of living arrangements.

The agencies that coordinate services of respite-care providers are likely to do so in one of two ways: 1) They allow qualified caretakers to provide service within their own home, or 2) they arrange for qualified caretakers to provide service in the home of the disabled individual.

The cost of respite care is usually paid by the parents or a supporting social agency. The idea of a sliding scale whereby parents and families pay only what they can afford and the agency picks up the remaining cost may also be found in some areas. The cost includes pay to the caretaker or agency providing the care, cost of coordinating services, and the cost of caring for the child for the designated period of time.

To find out about respite-care arrangements in your area, you should begin by contacting the program in which your child is already enrolled—his public school program, sheltered workshop program, or whatever. Your state mental health department, Division of Child and Family Services, or Division of Crippled Children's Services may also provide you with information regarding such programs. In some areas where respite-care arrangements have not been developed by organizations, parent groups have banded together to provide services. Look to your local parent groups to direct and inform you about the availability of respite-care services in your area.

It is important that you apply early for services. If you feel you would not need such services except in the case of emergency, we still urge you to apply early. By applying early you will have the opportunity to meet with the coordinators. In some cases you may even be able to meet with the direct-care person, and thus feel more comfortable when the time comes to leave your child.

Respite care has filled a pressing need for temporary care of disabled individuals. If you find that your community does not yet offer such services, discuss among your parent groups how you may be able to offer such services within your community. If agencies within your community do offer temporary arrangements such as those described, get to know where and how these services are provided so that if and when you find the need to use them you will feel comfortable doing so.

SUMMARY

We have discussed some important questions and issues in this chapter. Our purpose was not to pass judgment on your decisions, nor was it to invite the judgment of others on your decisions. Our purpose was to direct your thoughts to important aspects of your child's living arrangements, to offer alternatives that presently exist in communities regarding living arrangements, and to provide you with an organized method of reviewing these arrangements so that you, your family, and your child may best decide which one is ideal for you.

In an effort to direct your thoughts to the issues, we provided you with questions regarding the emotional and factual concerns involved in choosing among various living arrangements. Whether you are considering living separately from your child now or as a possibility at some time in the future, your greatest asset in making decisions will be the fact that you are well informed. It is our hope that we have provided you with the food for thought that will enable you to become well informed about the issues involved in making your decisions. To briefly review, the major issues we have addressed concern 1) you and your spouse's feelings about living separately from your child, 2) your handicapped child's feelings, 3) siblings' feelings, 4) the actual facts about your family situation that contribute to your decision, 5) the facts about your child's abilities and disabilities that contribute to your decision, 6) factors that affect the age at which you consider separate living arrangements, 7) the types of living arrangements that are available, and 8) the specific facts about a particular alternative home that make it an appropriate or inappropriate choice for your child.

We have included some comments that reflect our point of view on certain issues. These are intended to broaden the scope of your thinking to include concepts we have formed from our experiences working with other parents who have dealt with the question of living arrangements.

We are encouraged by the trend to continually improve the quality of life for handicapped citizens who are in residential care facilities. We are also impressed with changing parental attitudes that support keeping handicapped children at home. The decision about what is best for your child is a very personal one. As you learn the facts and deal openly with your feelings, answers will become evident to you. It will also become evident to you that regardless of your child's place of residence, he will always have the same place of importance in your lives.

10. FACTS VERSUS MYTHS ABOUT SPECIAL CHILDREN

Myth: All children who have _____ are _____.

Fact: We purposefully left this statement open-ended, for it is very likely that at some point in your child's development an educator, therapist, doctor, friend, or relative will fill in the blanks for you.

An example of this was related to us by a parent whose doctor stated, "All children who have cerebral palsy are retarded." Another example of this was given by an educator who pronounced, "All children with Down's syndrome are severely to moderately retarded." And yet another well-meaning friend reminded a parent, "All children who are hearing impaired are socially maladjusted."

Some of the above statements may appear to be obviously incorrect to you, others may be less so. We encourage you to be wary of any statement which implies that all children with a certain handicap are the same.

All children are different. All children who exhibit a specific handicap are also different. It has never been our experience to see two children respond to a specific handicap in exactly the same manner.

All children adjust to and compensate for handicaps in different ways. The only general statement we feel comfortable in making is that all children with the same handicap are different.

Myth: There is no purpose in educationally or vocationally training the profoundly or severely mentally handicapped individual.

Fact: There are many reasons why we should want to provide educational and/or vocational training to severely or profoundly mentally handicapped individuals. These reasons center less around economic factors and more around humanistic concerns.

Time and time again, however, we hear this statement made by medical and educational professionals, as well as by parents of nonhandicapped children. We have heard it expressed by those who are not familiar with severely or profoundly handicapped individuals. We have heard it from all sectors of society—legislators, business people, etc.

We have tried to state repeatedly that we would encourage every child, regardless of the handicapping condition, to lead as close to a normal life as it is possible for him to lead. This includes promoting and developing any skills a child has in an educational or vocational setting.

Sometimes, after many years of observation (by teachers, therapists, or counselors), professionals discover new skills not readily observable to parents or not easy to detect in a young child. There are many benefits from working with children regardless of the limitations they exhibit. These benefits include improved behavioral patterns in adults, increased opportunities for social interactions throughout life, and increased levels of independence in performing daily living skills (eating, dressing, and so forth).

Each child, regardless of the severity of his or her handicapping condition, should be exposed to the same experiences as other children and young adults who do not have handicaps.

Myth: Handicapped people cannot live independently.

Fact: Many handicapped adults can and do live independently. The type and severity of the handicap may be crucial issues to independent living. This is especially true of those who have severe mental handicaps. But what becomes even more important than the type or severity of an impairment is how the individual adjusts to or compensates for the handicap.

Many disabled individuals learn from their parents, relatives, and peers at an early age that socialization and independent living skills are critical issues. Parents and teachers attempt to foster increased independence, beginning with daily living skills (feeding, dressing, grooming), and slowly advance to more sophisticated judgment skills (cooking, shopping, maintaining a job). Social development is fostered in family life, social groups, school, and work experience. The ability to develop and use these skills in other situations does indeed determine the individual's potential for independent living.

A final point to be made is that recent technological and social advances have made independent living for the handicapped individual not only more possible but also more accessible. Examples of these technological changes include telephones for the deaf, hand-controlled cars, and barrier-free buildings, among others.

Social changes have occurred mainly because of the increased awareness of the public about handicapping conditions. This awareness can be noted in the media (television, newspapers) as well as in legislation (Public Law 94-142, barrier-free buildings). Yes, independent living is not only possible for handicapped adults, but also likely in many cases.

Myth: There is no schooling available for severely mentally handicapped (retarded) children.

Fact: A free public school education is available for all handicapped children from age three to age twenty-one, regardless of the type or severity of the handicapping condition. We have referred to Public Law 94-142, which includes this provision. If you have any questions regarding this, contact your local school district and request further information about this law and the programs available to you.

Myth: The term *brain damaged* is synonymous with *mentally retarded.*

Fact: The brain is highly specialized. That is, it contains millions of nerve cells which control all of the different body functions. Problem solving or learning is but a single function controlled by certain groups of cells in certain areas of the brain. A person may have brain damage confined to other cells or other areas of the brain not involved in learning. There are many types of brain damage that do not affect learning at all.

Myth: All people who have difficulty speaking (or cannot speak at all) are mentally handicapped.

Fact: As we have previously stated, speech and language handicaps may or may not be related to mental functioning. There are many bright and talented individuals who have tremendous speech and language handicaps.

Difficulties in communicating and/or using speech do not necessarily reflect a person's mental abilities. Such difficulties may be due to physical or neurological problems. There are times, however, when no physical or neurological problems can be found and yet speech and language impairment still exist.

In today's world, where media plays such an important role, we tend to look for people who are excellent speakers and attribute greater intellectual functioning to them. There are, however, many instances where people experience difficulties in speaking that are not due to mental handicaps.

Myth: Mentally handicapped (retarded) means unable to learn.

Fact: Mental handicap (retardation) has been surrounded by a number of myths and continues to be so. Educationally speaking, mentally handicapped individuals are not unable to learn, but rather they require different teaching methods, more time to learn, and (in some cases) may be limited in what they are able to learn.

It is important to remember that mental handicaps, like many handicapping conditions, are exhibited in a wide range of abilities. Mental handicaps range from profound to mild handicaps. The abilities and disabilities of mentally handicapped individuals likewise cover a wide range.

Mental handicap or retardation does not mean that a person cannot or will not learn.

Myth: My child must have certain skills to enter school. (For example, he must be toilet trained, have controllable behaviors, etc.).

Fact: Many educators and parents vividly remember when such a sad statement was true. We remember times when handicapped children were declared too retarded to enter school or too physically disabled to be enrolled in school. Indeed, if we were able to review the records of many handicapped individuals, such statements would appear in educational records.

No, a child need not be toilet trained before he enters school. Behavioral disorders are to be dealt with in the school, and management methods coordinated with home and family. The child who has a behavior problem should not be refused an appropriate program. A child cannot be denied a program due to lack of transportation to and from school.

Public Law 94-142 provides for the appropriate mainstreaming of all children. A physically handicapped child who can successfully fulfill academic requirements for a certain class may be qualified to be admitted to the class, regardless of his physically handicapping condition.

We would like to make a slight clarification here. Your child does not need to possess certain skills to be eligible for school; however, he may need to possess certain skills to be considered eligible for certain programs provided by your local school district. For example, when your child turns three there may be several programs (or preschool classes) that service your school district. It would be decided, based upon the specific skills your child demonstrates, which program (or class) would best service your child's needs. Thus it may be suggested that in view of your child's current abilities and disabilities he is eligible for a specific program.

Remember, however, that no handicapped child between three and twenty-one needs to exhibit certain skills in order to be considered eligible for school.

Myth: Children who are hospitalized or homebound for long periods of time due to illness have to miss out on their education.

Fact: Children who need to be absent from school for long periods of time due to illness, or who cannot attend public school at all because of a medical problem that confines them to home, are entitled to continue their education at home or in the hospital. This is usually accomplished through the combined efforts of a visiting tutor provided by the public school and a parent who follows through with the educational materials between tutoring sessions. If such services are needed, contact your local school district for information and guidance.

Myth: The life expectancy of all handicapped people is less than that of nonhandicapped people.

Fact: There are some handicapping conditions with accompanying medical problems that would lead to an early decline in general health and would shorten life expectancy. Other handicapping conditions, however, do not affect general health. If you have any questions about whether your child's handicapping condition could lead to a decline in general health that does not coincide with the normal aging process, you may want to question your physician.

Myth: Mentally handicapped adults are usually violent or sexually aggressive, and therefore people should fear them.

Fact: There is absolutely no factual basis for this statement. Some mentally handicapped people lack judgment about what is socially acceptable behavior. Often this lack of judgment is misinterpreted as being "aggressive" or "violent." There is no reason to fear or avoid a mentally handicapped person.

Myth: All people who have paralysis below the waist are sexually impaired.

Fact: Paralysis is most often due to nerve damage. There are, however, many different nerves that go to different body parts. No general statement can be made regarding this; each case is individual. The determining factors would be where the nerve damage is located and exactly what nerves are involved. In many cases a person's hips and legs may be affected and sexual functioning left totally intact. Your physician (perhaps a neurologist) may be able to provide counseling regarding your particular case.

Myth: The cause for a handicapping condition can always be identified.

Fact: There are many handicapping conditions for which no cause can be determined. There may be no significant factors in the child's medical background or parents' history. Pregnancy and delivery may have been without incident. Medical tests may all be negative. While certain handicapping conditions are known to result from certain causes, others result from causes which medical professionals are currently unable to identify.

Myth: If you have given birth to one handicapped child, chances are greater that you will have another.

Fact: Handicapping conditions result from various reasons. As explained above, some of these reasons remain unknown. Some handicaps result from genetic factors, which may alter the likelihood of other offspring being affected. If you have any doubts about your or your spouse's genetic background, we would suggest genetic counseling, which can be arranged through your physician.

In addition to genetic studies, there are medical tests that can be done during pregnancy to rule out certain handicapping conditions. Examples are ultrasound and amniocentesis. It should be noted that only certain conditions can be detected with these tests.

If you have concerns about another child being born with a handicap, we suggest you discuss them with your physician. He may or may not think that genetic counseling and/or testing is indicated in your particular case.

Myth: If handicapped people marry and have children, their children will be handicapped.

Fact: The myth in this statement is that it does not apply in general to all couples. Each couple would need to investigate their own medical background. People from whom you should seek information may include the families of both spouses, your family physicians, your obstetrician-gynecologist, and a genetic counselor.

SUMMARY

The statements we have selected are representative of the kinds of myths that exist about handicapped people. It is possible that you have heard similar statements in your encounters with people who have preconceived notions.

We have included this section in order to draw your attention to the differences between myths and facts.

We have, in another section, discussed the difference between medical facts and opinions. We encouraged you to distinguish between them in an effort to identify what is actually true about your child and what is conjecture. Myths, unlike opinions, are not based on conjecture, but on mistaken ideas.

Myths develop from prejudices, fears, lack of information, or incorrect information. Some myths are based on past circumstances that no longer exist. We encourage you to distinguish between myths and facts in an effort to identify what is fact and what is fallacy.

11. FINANCIAL CONSIDERATIONS

In the last few years, advances in legislation and education have helped to ease the financial burden of raising a handicapped child. Unfortunately, this is not true for every family. The additional cost involved in raising your special child will be dependent upon your own financial position, your child's handicapping condition (can he support himself), the area in which you live, and your child's age.

Finding out what financial opportunities you are entitled to may be difficult and may involve a great deal of time. In talking with parents it became evident to us that regardless of the financial situation, people need to investigate public and private programs (insurance, supplemental governmental aid, welfare) which provide assistance to families. Many programs have supplemental as well as total assistance. Families have related to us that once they determined their own needs, they were able to find an appropriate financial program.

INSURANCE

Jeffrey was diagnosed as being hypertonic. The muscles in his legs would often become very tight and he would be unable to move them effectively. Jeff could not sit well, but could move his arms if he was supported the right way. Because he needed help in sitting, his physical therapist and doctor discussed with Mr. and Mrs. B. the idea of getting him a special wheelchair. The B.'s were anxious to do this,

135

but feared the cost involved would be prohibitive. They met with a representative from the medical-supply company and were shocked at the prices of wheelchairs. Even with Mr. B.'s healthy income, they could not absorb the cost. The sales representative suggested that they check out Mr. B.'s company's insurance policy before deciding against the chair. In doing so, Mr. B. discovered that the insurance company would not only pay for Jeff's chair, but would also pay for Jeff's physical therapy—a cost that until that point the B.'s were paying on their own.

Just as all insurance companies are different, so are the policies they issue. The benefits you are entitled to will differ from one type of policy to another. As in the case of the B.'s, it is important for you to know your policy and exactly what it provides.

In reviewing your policy, be sure that you note the definition of *dependent*. At what age and under what circumstances will your children no longer be considered dependents? Will there be some future time when your child will require an independent policy? What will the cost of such a policy be? Would it be more financially sound to accept federal or state moneys for medical care?

Check to see if your child is still covered under your policy even if he is living in a residential program. Note the terms of the policy regarding respite care (or any other statements regarding temporary care). Talk with the directors of your child's residential care facility to determine if private medical insurance is indeed necessary. If you are prepared and ask questions, you will find that financial arrangements usually can be made.

Many parents are confused by the language in their policy. If this is the case, get to know your insurance representative. Inform him of the special circumstances in your family, and determine what types of benefits may pertain to you. Certainly not every special medical need can be anticipated, but if you are aware of what your insurance provides for, it may alleviate many problems in the future.

Insurance companies generally provide for two basic types of coverage. Group coverage is what many companies and businesses hold. The companies pay insurance premiums for all their employees and sometimes (for a small fee to the employee) for employees' dependents. Because group insurance programs cover a large number and variety of people, rates tend to be lower and benefits tend to be better than individual policies.

People subscribe to individual policies as either a primary mode of insurance or to supplement existing policies. If for some reason your company does not provide group coverage (perhaps it is too small, or you are self-employed) you may want to seek out an individual medical insurance policy. Such policies tend to be more costly; however, they may be written more specifically for your needs.

Having adequate insurance coverage is a high priority among many of the families we see. If your child is covered under an insurance policy, be sure to check the benefits. Find out what will be paid for and what will not. Get to know your agent and ask about unclear points within your policy. As in the case of the B.'s, it may be essential information.

HEALTH MAINTENANCE ORGANIZATIONS (HMO)

An alternative to conventional health insurance is belonging to a health maintenance organization (HMO). An HMO is an organization set up to provide complete medical care and coverage to its members at extremely low rates. When a person joins an HMO he is charged a set fee (monthly or annually). For this fee he is provided with complete medical care by doctors and hospitals affiliated with the HMO.

HMOs are growing rapidly throughout the country. They are not designed to be "socialized medicine" or a clinic; rather their function is to provide comprehensive medical care. In doing so, they attempt to lower the cost of health care by 1) maintaining the overall health of their members (through regular checkups, immunizations, etc.), and 2) providing low-cost medical coverage for their members.

HMOs, unlike most insurance programs, include in their coverage such services (paid in full) as doctors' office visits, periodic physicials, immunizations and inoculations, well-baby care, laboratory tests, and hospital charges. In order to receive these and similar services, however, members must use a doctor and facility affliated with the HMO.

Commonly, doctors affliated with the HMO practice under one roof—within the HMO. Some, however, also continue private practice in a different office. The member could then choose the preferred setting for an appointment. The same is true for hospitals affliated with HMOs.

The total fee for outpatient services, unlike conventional insurances, is not based on a percentage. The HMO plan covers such costs in full. It also covers hospital room and board, hospital charges, extended-care facilities, and emergency services. Other services—

such as prescription drugs, medical equipment, and psychiatric consultations—are provided for members at costs usually lower than they would be under regular insurance plans.

Currently many companies offer employees a choice of conventional insurance plans or HMOs. For those who choose HMOs, a flat monthly payment by the employee would be required, with the company paying the balance. For many families this flat charge is incredibly less than their total monthly medical bills. For this reason, many HMOs are thriving.

It is also possible in some areas to join an HMO on your own. Naturally, your monthly payment would be substantially more than a company-subsidized plan, but your yearly medical costs may still be reduced. In some areas HMOs are growing so rapidly that they have had to shut the doors to new independent subscribers. If this is the case in your area, keep trying. Once the organization adds additional staff and facilities they usually reopen their doors.

HMOs may or may not be a new concept to you. In some areas of the nation they have caught on quickly—even to the point of providing insurance companies with competition. In other areas they may be just getting started or have not begun at all. If the organization appears to be of interest to you, contact your local health department to find the HMO in your area. As in any other health plan, you will probably want to check out the facilities, doctors' qualifications, services, etc. For many families HMOs may be the medical care program they need.

TAXES

It is likely that you will be eligible for special deductions and credits if your family has incurred outstanding medical, dental, educational, or special care expenses throughout the year. It is also possible that you may qualify for other tax benefits because of special items and/or equipment you may have purchased or special transportation costs you have incurred. To determine which deductions and/or credits you are eligible for, it is important that you seek out professional help.

Much of this help can come directly from the government, free of charge. Yearly the IRS publishes a toll-free phone number to help you to fill out your tax return and answer special questions. Take advantage of this number. No record is kept of your name, address, or Social Security number if you call. Special publications are also available from the IRS. These publications are easy to understand and are free of charge. You may request them by writing the IRS, 6000 Manchester Trafficway Terrace, Kansas City, Missouri, 64120, or by calling your local IRS office. Be sure to specifically request the publications that cover child and disabled dependent care, medical and dental expenses, and highlights of the tax changes for the year. If you have other specific circumstances—for example, if you have made specific contributions or have incurred child care expenses—request publications that relate to those items also. Because laws change quickly, it is important that you make these requests yearly to keep informed about annual changes. You should also keep careful records of all your financial transactions.

Mary D., age fourteen, lives at home with her mother and grandmother. Mary is mentally handicapped and attends a special school during the day. Mary's parents were divorced and her mother, a registered nurse, is required to work swing shifts in the evening. Because Mary is unable to care for herself, when her mother worked such late hours her grandmother cared for her. There was a weekly wage agreed upon between Mrs. D. and her mother for the service. At income tax time, Mrs. D. was confused about how to deduct Mary's child care expenses. She contacted the IRS and was told that changes in the laws regarding work-related expenses had taken place. Whereas last year she could not deduct Mary's child care because a live-in relative was the caretaker, this year she could.

For tax purposes, it is a good idea to keep careful records regarding all your expenses. As in Mrs. D.'s case, had she not retained her check stubs, she would not have proof of paying her mother for child care services during the previous year. Being organized will help, but regardless, be sure to demand receipts for all your expenses.

As we have already stated, tax laws change from year to year, and some changes may affect you. Keep informed about annual changes either by contacting the IRS in writing or phone or by contacting a reputable accountant or attorney. Guard against taking the advice of "Uncle Bill" —talk to someone who knows. Take the time to keep careful records throughout the year so that you can take advantage of tax breaks at the end of the year.

SOCIAL SECURITY

There are many factors which are considered by the Social Security Administration in determining benefits and moneys available to you and your child. It is difficult to make general statements as to who is eligible and who is not, at what age a child becomes eligible, and the amount of money which may be received from Social Security. For these reasons, we strongly encourage you to contact the local office of the Social Security Administration and request information regarding Social Security and Supplemental Security Income.

Social Security benefits are provided by the government as a result of contributions made throughout your working life. The amount of moneys and the extent of benefits are dependent not only upon your specific contributions, but also upon the current legislative status of Social Security.

A person who works and earns Social Security benefits does so for himself and also for his family. Among the factors that determine when and how much is proivded by Social Security are age, disability, family income, and the length of time you worked.

Supplemental Security Income (SSI) is a program administered by the Social Security Administration, but this program should not be confused with regular Social Security. Those who qualify for SSI receive additional moneys from the government to supplement their present level of income. Eligibility for the program can be best identified at your Social Security Administration's local office, but it is important to note that children as well as adults may qualify.

As a parent of a disabled child, it will be important for you to contact your local office and investigate all of the programs and benefits available to your child. It is also important that you obtain a Social Security number for your child at an early age.

Social Security benefits may, as we have said, take the form of supplemental support, or they may be total support. Such benefits may be available immediately or at a later age for your child. Contact to your local office may be made by phone, in writing, or in person. Not only is such information crucial in determining your present financial situation, but it may also be beneficial in planning for your child's financial future.

PUBLIC ASSISTANCE

Public assistance programs exist, in some form, throughout the United States. Many, although administered at the state level, are dependent at least in part on federal assistance. Such programs often include specific assistance programs as well as general payment provisions.

Your family or child may qualify for specific financial assistance without being considered a total welfare recipient. In other words, if you need to obtain financial assistance for a specific purpose which is not covered by your medical insurance, you may be able to receive such a predetermined amount from your state public assistance program.

This assistance may also be found in your state for special medical attention (including food for special diets, drugs, or therapists). Again, determining if you are eligible and how much assistance your state provides must be done by contacting your local public assistance office and relating your financial situation to a case worker.

Determining what is available in your state may also help you to plan for your child's financial future. By speaking with the people presently involved in working with your child (social workers, teachers, therapists, work supervisors) and contacting your state public assistance office you will obtain the facts necessary to better prepare and plan for your child's future.

Some parents have related to us that they had a great deal of difficulty in finding the appropriate office to provide them with the necessary information regarding public assistance. In some states governmental assistance programs are referred to as Crippled Children Services. This is not to say that your child need have a physically crippling disability, but that he may qualify for programs within this division based on any one of a number of handicapping conditions. These programs are usually administered through your state's Department of Health, but they may also be administered under the state's Department of Education or Department of Welfare. To find out more about your state's public assistance programs, contact the social worker in your child's present program (school, residential facility, or sheltered workshop). If your child is not currently enrolled in a program, contact your state departments of health, education, and welfare.

SOCIAL SERVICE AGENCIES

Many civic groups and social service organizations provide services to handicapped children and their families. Such services range from very special and specific care to general care and support.

They may provide medical, educational, or social assistance. Some groups are religiously based, others are not. Some groups narrow their assistance to special handicapping conditions, others do not. It is probable that within your community a civic group exists that would be willing to offer aid to your child, or children like yours, in any one of a number of ways.

Examples of such civic and fraternal organizations are the Shriners, Lions, Elks, and the Rotary clubs. Religious groups are exemplified by the Jewish Federation, Catholic Charities, and the Lutheran Welfare Services. Many colleges and universities also have special clinics or arrangements made within their dental and medical schools. There are private foundations and social service organizations (such as United Way and Easter Seals), which also offer special assistance. You can contact such services by referring to "Social Service Organizations" listed in your phone directory.

Although many of these organizations (Elks, Lions, etc.) provide specific services to handicapped children, some do not. If they do not already have such programs, do not hesitate to make such needs known to them. Many organizations welcome suggestions on how they can aid the community, and are willing to work on an individual basis as well as with parent organizations.

EDUCATIONAL/VOCATIONAL TRAINING

The passage of Public Law 94-142 brought tremendous financial relief to parents with respect to education. Before the passage of this law, many parents had been shouldering the cost of their handicapped child's education. This cost came in the form of private school placements (when public school placements were unavailable), special therapies (physical, occupational, or speech), transportation, and specialized educational testing. Because such costs were likely to be prohibitive to many families, many handicapped children suffered.

With the new law, however, the cost of your handicapped child's education falls directly on the public school system. As noted previously, your child is entitled to a free and appropriate education. This means that you no longer have to pay for special classes, therapies, testing, and transporting of your child between the ages of three and twenty-one.

For many handicapped children, however, education needs to begin before the age of three and extend after the age of twenty-one. Many states do not provide for such extensive services. There are, however, many federal, county, and township organizations as well as private nonprofit organizations and private for-profit practices that do offer such services.

Federal and state organizations that provide services usually do so for minimal to no fee. The Comprehensive Employment Training Act (CETA) project is an example of such an organization. It uses part of its moneys to train handicapped citizens in specific areas for competitive employment. Youth Employment and Training Programs (YETP) as well as other title programs are other examples of such services. Access and information to such programs can be made by contacting your public school social worker or counselor before your child turns twenty-one. If your child is over twenty-one you can obtain information by writing to the U.S. Office of Education, Bureau of the Handicapped, 400 Maryland Avenue, S.W., Washington, DC, 20202. Involvement in such programs as CETA and YETP often provides the handicapped person with skills that are marketable in employment, thus easing some of the financial concern.

Private nonprofit organizations are run at the local, county, or state level. They are financed by government and state subsidizing, private donations, and by charging fees or tuition. Usually fees are based on a sliding-scale formula. This means that the tuition cost to each family is based on the family's ability to pay for such services. Therefore, of families receiving the same services, one family may pay fifty dollars a month, while another family may pay one hundred dollars a month.

Private nonprofit organizations provide such services as infant-stimulation programs, sheltered workshops, vocational training, and social activities. Some organizations are now also beginning to provide day care services for children with special needs. Contact your local school district, social service agency, or clergy to learn about such programs in your area.

Private practices and clinics are another alternative for educational and vocational training for children under the age of three and over the age of twenty-one. Although many good practices exist, they can be quite costly and, for some families, unnecessary. If you are considering such a program, examine it carefully. Look to see what specific equipment it has, the quality of the staff, and the programming it offers. Be wary of private practices that "overtest" or run many tests of the same type. Question if they want to repeat testing already in your child's file and determine if it is necessary to do so. Compare private programs to those which may be available to you publicly. While some families find a definite need for private practices and programs, others do not. To find out about private practice programs in your area, it is best to have someone refer you to them. Therapists, teachers, social workers, doctors, and clergy may all be able to help you find a reputable private practice program.

Most private for-profit programs do not operate sliding fee scales. All testing, therapies, and evaluations are done at a fixed price. The cost of such services, as we have mentioned, can run fairly high. Be certain that you investigate which (if any) of these services would be covered by your private insurance. You may also explore a fixed payment schedule with the clinic or agency from whom you are receiving the services.

LOOKING TO THE FUTURE

How can I financially provide for my handicapped child after I am gone? Who can I trust to take care of his financial and physical well-being? These are difficult questions that many parents face. The more dependent their child appears to remain on them, the more difficult the question becomes. As your child grows, the limitations of his handicap may become more evident. Probably the older the child is, the more you are aware of what he can and cannot do. If you are aware that he will remain dependent, the question of "What will happen when..?" may be even more painful.

Many parents seek out competent legal advice regarding their wills and trust funds for their handicapped child. There are many ways a will or trust fund can be executed so that your child will be well cared for. Make certain that your lawyer is aware of your special circumstances. Be certain that you look realistically at your plans, taking into account financial considerations, inflation, rising medical costs, and your child's special needs.

Robert is a thrity-two-year-old mentally handicapped citizen. Robert's parents passed away thirteen years ago and left Robert with a trust fund. At that time Robert was in a residential private nonprofit facility. During the day he attended a nearby workshop and was paid minimum wage—not nearly enough to support himself or his cost of living in the residential care facility. Robert's family had set what they thought would be a sizable income from the trust fund, but over the last thirteen years, due to inflation and rising medical costs, the income has become insufficient. Robert's social worker, aware of his position, was actually anxious to spend the last of Robert's money and apply for public assistance. In dollars and cents, Robert would collect more on public assistance then he currently does on his trust fund.

Inflation and rising medical costs had greatly diminished Robert's monthly income from the fund. Although his residential home provided for most of his needs, there were many special trips that Robert could not participate in. There were many times when his clothing purchases had to be restricted to essentials, and many services public aid offered which Robert was unable to receive. Robert's parents had not counted on such a consistent and rapid rise in expenses. Eventually the ideal financial situation was worked out for Robert, but it was not the plan Robert's parents originally had intended.

There are many cases where families have planned well for their children. There are families who—regardless of their financial resources—have provided for a handicapped child by being prepared and knowledgeable. This knowledge includes knowing about state and federal assistance programs as well as recognizing personal financial resources. It has been our experience that parents who are knowledgeable and plan ahead will be able to provide well for their handicapped child regardless of their personal finances.

12. DEVELOPING A GOOD SELF-IMAGE

Your child's self-image will have a tremendous impact on his overall success and happiness. A child who feels good about himself is a self-motivated child.

Unlike other areas of development that can be measured through testing, the development of self-image cannot be measured objectively. It is therefore difficult to judge whether or not we are successful in helping children to feel good about themselves.

In this section we will discuss factors that contribute to a positive self-image: self-respect, self-confidence, a feeling of worthiness, a good body image, and pride.

The parental role in providing the foundation upon which these feelings are built is critical. The example parents set by treating their child in a manner that fosters a positive self-image will establish the pattern for others to treat him similarly.

We realize that there are varying degrees of handicapping conditions. We believe, however, that all children, regardless of the severity and type of their handicapping conditions, develop a self-image—feelings about who they are and how they think others perceive them. Whether a handicapping condition is severely, moderately, or mildly limiting; whether it is physical, mental, or both; every child deserves to be treated in such a way as to let him know he is a valuable human being. Such treatment leads to the self-realization that this is so.

The suggestions we make in this section have built-in assumptions that every child perceives himself in some way, and that he draws some conclusions about how others perceive him. Until we know a great deal more about the workings of the mind and exactly how and what is processed at various levels of maturity, we feel we must make these assumptions. The suggestions, therefore, apply to all handicapped children regardless of their levels of maturity. Differences will exist in how you apply certain suggestions because of particular handicaps. Such differences will be pointed out later in the chapter.

SELF-RESPECT

A child who is treated with respect develops a sense of self-respect. People often unknowingly rob handicapped children of the respect due them. At times this happens for reasons of expediency. Other times it is assumed a child does not understand what is going on. Even in an effort to help a child, we often misplace our priorities concerning his need to be treated with respect.

The following suggestions are based upon situations we have seen in which people seemed rather insensitive to handicapped children's feelings. We hope they will serve to help make you aware of how you can become more sensitive to treating your child with the respect he deserves.

1. Accord your child as much privacy as you would naturally allow anyone else. Toileting, changing of clothing, and other personal hygiene should be done in an enclosed area with only those present who are needed for physical assistance. This should be enforced at home, in school, and at other public places, particularly with older children. In addition to the privacy one deserves for self-care, all people are entitled to some private moments—moments when they can be alone without others infringing. Small children commonly use such private time when they are left alone to look at, listen to, and touch things they are interested in. Babies often coo and make pleasurable sounds during these private moments, indicating a feeling of comfort and contentment. Older children commonly choose to be in a private room without being disturbed to do whatever it is they enjoy doing: listening to music, watching television, or just resting. All people deserve to have both their physical and mental privacy respected.

2. Trust your child to handle information about his handicapping condition. Explain it to him as you did to others, being as realistic and honest as possible. Denying or ignoring his handicap may imply to him that it is something to be ashamed of. Knowing you understand and accept his differences will help him to better understand, accept, and respect his own differences as well as others' differences.

3. When discussing your child with others, acknowledge his presence if he is within hearing distance. That is, do not talk as though he is not there or say anything you would not want him to hear. If you are discussing something that pertains to him and he is capable of contributing to the discussion, encourage his participation. Be aware also of not discussing issues openly about your child that would cause him embarrassment or humiliation. Whether he is present or not, there are some things in every person's life that are best kept private. If you do not think your child would want something pertaining to him known publicly, do not discuss it openly. Everyone should have some choice as to what personal information he wants to share with others. If your child cannot express that choice, it is up to you to determine what information he may or may not want to share without sacrificing his self-respect.

4. If your child is a victim of remarks, stares, and/or pity, make certain insofar as possible that he understands that the problem belongs to those who exhibit such behavior and not to him. Your response need not necessarily be an angry one unless something was obviously meant to insult your child. A simple explanation about the lack of education and understanding of others should alleviate his own discomfort. If he is unable to deal directly with others' inappropriate responses to his handicap, you may want to deal with it yourself. If, however, he is capable of dealing with it, do not deny him the chance to develop greater self-respect. Allow him to deal with it himself.

5. When things are to be done to your child, particularly by medical people, explain what is to be done, how it may make him feel, and how long it will take. Do not simply take over his body without showing him that you respect his right to know what is to be done.

6. Handle accidental occurrences which may cause embar-

rassment as quietly and unnoticeably as possible. Such things as spilling of food, falling, and so forth should elicit the necessary assistance with as few words as possible. What you do say should indicate your concern about your child rather than the incident—"Are you all right?" or "You seem fine."

7. Whenever possible, approach your child at eye level. That is, do not always stand over him when speaking to him. If he is not at eye level with you, either lower yourself or raise him. If he is in a group, make certain he is not always physically lower than others, as may be the case if he is unable to stand. Join him at his level (sit next to him) so that others become aware of including him on an "equal" basis.

These few suggestions can serve to alert you to experiences that handicapped people are often subject to and over which they may have little control. It is up to you as parents to establish a precedent for others who have contact with your child. Whether or not you think he fully understands appropriate moral and social behavior, he should always be accorded the respect and dignity due him. One cannot measure embarrassment or humiliation in terms of age levels. We must assume that all people are capable of experiencing such feelings. Taking every precaution to insure that handicapped children are not helpless victims of those who simply are not sensitive at times, and demanding that they be treated respectfully, will help them develop a sense of self-respect.

SELF-CONFIDENCE

An integral part of self-image is confidence. Children must learn to trust themselves. They must trust their ability to achieve success. They must trust their ability to make choices. They must trust their ability to relate to others—to be likable. Again, a great deal will depend on you. Usually the degree of confidence a child develops in himself is directly related to the amount of confidence parents and family members have in him.

In the section on discipline we discussed several factors as they related to appropriate behavior: 1) placing realistic demands on your child, 2) applying the same rules to him as you do to your other children, 3) rewarding and punishing him appropriately, 4) allowing him to deal with human imperfections. By doing these things you not only teach appropriate behavior, but also convey your trust in your child. When children are expected to do certain things, the message implied is, "They would not expect something of me if I really could not do it. I must be capable of meeting their expectations."

Your trust and confidence in your child will become his trust and confidence in himself. If you pity him, if you are afraid he cannot succeed, he will probably feel pitiful and afraid to try. Suggestions for instilling trust and self-confidence include:

1. Do not be physically overprotective. Encourage your child to try whatever it is he feels capable of doing and whatever you feel he may be able to do. To cite just a few examples of people who have been given the opportunity to try, there is a ski club whose members each have one leg, a blind entertainer who plays golf, blind and deaf competitors in the martial arts, as well as a wheelchair-bound karate champion. The Special Olympics is a success story for every child who participates each year. To fall down and get up seems far better than never to have fallen down.

2. Do not be mentally overprotective. Do not solve problems, provide answers, or make any choices for your child if he is in any way capable of doing so himself. Allow him extra time if he needs it to deliberate. Do not speak for him. Give him the chance to communicate with others even if he has difficulty making himself understood. Ask his opinion when appropriate. Provide mental challenges in which you believe he can experience success. Do not work down to his level, but encourage him to rise to the challenge.

3. Do not be emotionally overprotective. Referring again to how others may respond inappropriately to your child, he not only needs to deal with this situation to maintain his self-respect, but he also needs to deal with his feelings. If you feel sorry for him, he will no doubt begin to feel sorry for himself. Trust him not only to respond to others, but also to handle the emotions such encounters elicit. Words of encouragment, not pity, are needed. There is a well-known singer who stutters when he speaks. When he appears in public, he often makes humorous references to his manner of speaking. Humor can be a positive tool that can replace self-pity when someone sees himself as different. Many comedians have capitalized on their physical differences. Also, do not interfere in your child's disagree-ments. Allow him to handle his own problems with others.

Whether he is emotionally mature or immature for his age, he will deal on the level where he is able to cope and others will learn to adapt and relate to him.

Letting go is a sign that you do in fact have confidence in your child to make responsible decisions. At times all children make the wrong decisions. Parents often feel more hurt than their children when decisions result in disappointment. It takes a great deal of courage to stand by and watch a child learn from his own mistakes. Your confidence in your child's ability to succeed, regardless of stumbling blocks, will be the basis for the self-confidence he develops.

SELF-WORTH

Feelings of worthiness to a great extent center around one's ability to give of himself to others. People who feel they are always on the receiving end often develop feelings of worthlessness. On the other hand, people who feel they are contributing something of themselves to others feel needed and worthwhile.

Suggestions for helping your child develop a feeling of worthiness will again be similar to those made in the section on discipline. Here again, as in developing self-confidence, the emphasis is not on appropriate behavior, but on the feelings developed by being a contributing member of society.

1. Let your child know that his achievements give you joy. No matter how minimal an achievement, acknowledge it. Let your child know that both his effort and his success are a source of happiness to you.
2. Do not always wait for achievements. Take opportunities to show your appreciation for your child for just being the special person that he is. Unexpected hugs and kisses will add to his sense of worthiness.
3. Expect and demand as much independence as your child is capable of achieving. Convey to him that he is able. His accomplishments do not always depend on your help. He is worthwhile all by himself.
4. Find ways for your child to contribute. Sharing household tasks, caring for pets, watering a plant to make it grow, sending a greeting card to a friend, making a picture for the wall, all help to make things more enjoyable for others.

People who feel that the quality of life around them is somehow improved or enriched because of their presence tend to feel worthwhile.

BODY IMAGE

Your child's body image will be determined by his grooming, personal hygiene, and overall physical appearance. It is our opinion that this very personal picture one has of his body has less to do with well-formed limbs or features and more to do with how much care is given to his body. A child may have "perfect" features and a physically sound body. If parents take no time for good care for his body, however, he will soon begin to think they do not take pride in his body and eventually will assume the same attitude himself. It is doubtful that such a child would become an attractive adult. The parent who takes time to care for a child's body will convey a message of pride in that child's physical attributes and will no doubt produce a well-groomed, attractive adult.

Nonhandicapped as well as handicapped children often need assistance with the finer points of grooming. We consider grooming activities the one exception we would make to the rule of withholding assistance. When it comes to grooming, we feel that the quality of the result should take precedence over demanding total independence. We suggest you provide the assistance that is needed to help him look his best—hairstyling and makeup, for example. Be cautious when providing this assistance, however, not to diminish your child's sense of independence. It can be done very matter-of-factly and be treated as a source of enjoyment for you, since most parents do enjoy primping and fussing over a child's appearance.

Suggestions for hygiene and grooming include the following:
1. Oral hygiene (brushing of teeth) should be done thoroughly several times a day, particularly with children on medication or special diets.
2. Shaving, deodorant, makeup, colognes, etc., can be introduced at appropriate ages.
3. Hairstyles should be flattering, not merely easy to care for.
4. Clothing should fit well, be flattering, and age appropriate.
5. Weight should be controlled.
6. Good posture, head held high and shoulders back, should be encouraged for those who are physically able.

7. Braces, prostheses, wheelchairs, or other adaptive devices and equipment that are worn or used in moving about should be kept as clean as possible.

It is realistic to say that if your child's handicapping conditions affects him physically, it will indeed be a part of his body image. However, body image as it relates to the total self-image is not necessarily based on what one sees when he looks into the mirror. Certainly blind people have body images of themselves and of others as well. The issue seems to be one of placing value on the physical aspect of one's being. If you teach a child to care *for* his body, he will learn to care *about* his body and see it as valuable.

PRIDE

Feelings of pride result from a combination of all the factors we have already discussed. The child who has a sense of self-respect, feels worthwhile, has self-confidence and a positive body image will develop pride in himself. He will see himself as a special person. His attitude will be, "I am important. I want the best for myself." This is not selfish pride, but rather a deserving pride. It involves a reward for being a unique and special human being—not special in the sense of being handicapped, but special in the sense of possessing the qualities we have discussed. If you have helped your child develop these qualities, he is likely to be a proud person.

There is, however, another view we take of pride. It involves the ability to exercise one's importance and to get what one deserves.

Although tremendous gains have been made to insure the rights of handicapped citizens, there is still some discrimination evident in our society. Parents of handicapped children and those who work with them owe it to them to work toward eliminating these social and physical barriers. Only by doing so can they insure that the sense of pride they have helped their children to develop will be preserved by society.

The task begins within your family and extends beyond to all those who would knowingly or by chance, deny your child any of the rights he deserves. Suggestions for preserving the proud image you are developing in your child include:

1. Start breaking down the architectural barriers that exclude him. Anyplace he wants to go or is capable of being should be proud to have him. If you plan to go to a movie, restaurant, bowling alley, theater, beach, church, or concert, call beforehand and make certain the place is accessi-

ble to your child. If it is not, speak to people in management and express your needs. Request changes.

2. Teach your child to compete where competition is appropriate. Whether it is a small school event or an important job for which he is suited and able, encourage healthy competition. He is already aware of his handicapping condition. Make him extremely proud of his strengths and abilities.

3. Encourage an assertive attitude. A proud person speaks up for what he wants and for what is rightfully his. This begins at a very young age when you offer him choices and encourage him to indicate his preferences. It develops further as he learns to work for rewards he wants. If a reward he earns is denied him, teach him to assert himself in order to get it. A proud person does not allow others to take advantage of him. He is not passive when his basic rights are denied. He is actively involved in getting what is best for him.

SEVERELY HANDICAPPED CHILDREN

As previously stated, there are cases of severely limiting handicapping conditions where our suggestions may need to be adapted. The basic ideas, however, hold true regardless of the severity and type of the handicapping condition. In applying suggestions to your particular child, we would offer the following food for thought.

There are times we have no way of knowing how aware a severely handicapped child is of his experiences. Whether a child is fully, partially, or not at all aware, we believe he deserves to be treated with the utmost respect. It is our opinion that suggestions made in the area of self-respect apply as written to *all* children.

In the section on self-confidence we talked about letting go. How do you let go of a severely handicapped child? How does he manage on his own? Letting go does not necessarily mean removing needed assistance. It means allowing growth to take place. In the case of a severely handicapped child, the only letting go possible may mean separation from your direct care. It may mean leaving him with a qualified sibling, relative, or sitter where he must learn to relate to others on his own. It may mean allowing qualified teachers and therapists to work with him in their own way, using their own approach while you are not present. By letting go in this way he learns that others besides you will place demands on him, and also will grow to love him for the person that he is. As a parent you cannot realistically control everything that happens to your child. For this reason he should develop the confidence to relate to others using whatever is available from within himself.

In the section on self-worth we discussed achievement and contribution. It is our experience that even the most severely handicapped children are able to achieve and contribute. Achievement may mean turning to a noise, holding up one's head, or making a sound. Contribution may be a passive involvement in making a greeting card, the joy of his achievement, or simply his presence. A child's mere inclusion in the process of contributing to others can develop his feeling of worthiness as a participating family member.

Pride and dignity, like self-respect, are again something every child deserves. In the case of the child who cannot assert himself, it is up to you to see that your child is treated as an equal, and to make certain that provisions are made by others so he can have as full a life as he is capable of living. As his spokesperson, you will need to establish a place of importance for him in places he goes and among people with whom he comes in contact.

THE IMPORTANCE OF REINFORCEMENT

A thought that has occurred to many of us who work with handicapped children is that we sometimes tend to tarnish the positive self-image we are trying to develop. In our attempt to stimulate continual progress, we often fail to give a child adequate time to experience his successes. The moment a skill is mastered, we feel compelled to immediately move on to a new challenge. By doing so, we are placing minor emphasis on what he is able to do and major emphasis on what he is unable to do. For example, if we have been working to teach a child to crawl, and after several months he begins to crawl independently, we begin one week later to work on teaching him to walk. If we want our children to develop a lasting positive self-image, it is critical that we allow plenty of time for them to enjoy their successes. Nonhandicapped children instinctively take time by themselves to enjoy newly learned skills before they move on to more difficult ones. We need not rush on to the next task that a child is unable to do. We encourage that when a goal in a particular area of development is achieved, some time should follow during which no new goal is introduced—time that is used solely for the positive reinforcement of success.

BONDING

It was difficult to decide where in this section to discuss the subject of bonding. It is the beginning and the end, the bottom line, so to speak, in the development of self-image. We decided to make it our final point; if we leave you with no other thought about developing a positive self-concept, we would hope that this one point will remain with you.

Bonding refers to the natural feeling of security and trust that develops in the parent-child relationship. It is literally the bond that is formed between parent and child, the basis for the inner security the child will feel as he continues to mature.

The subject of bonding is a difficult one to approach when working with parents. Although we feel we must talk about it, because it is the very foundation for the development of a child's positive self-image, many parents seem uncomfortable during the discussion. They feel that bonding should have taken place naturally since they love their children. Some parents resent our questioning whether or not it has in fact taken place.

Although bonding is a natural process, it does not always just happen. Realistically speaking, there are many factors that can disrupt the process. For example, the death or illness of a loved one prior to or soon after the birth of a baby can affect a parent's reactions to the baby.

In the case of a handicapped child, during the initial acceptance process some parents often need time to deal with their own feelings of insecurity, and therefore cannot relate as well as they would have to the "normal" baby they were expecting.

There are cases where children are colicky and parents feel they can do nothing to comfort them. The inability to comfort a child who appears to be in distress can give one a strong feeling of parental insecurity, which is conveyed to the child.

Some handicapped children are difficult to hold. They seem to always be pulling away or withdrawing from parental attempts to be physically close. Although this is not intentional, parents often find it difficult to develop a feeling of closeness with such children.

It is important to realize that you cannot equate bonding with love. A parent may love a child very much and yet not develop a bond with that child. Bonding involves not only a feeling of love, but also feelings of ease, comfort, and security that come with the handling and care of a child. Your confidence and security are conveyed to your child through the pleasure he derives from your touch, and they become his own feelings of comfort and security.

It is easy to see how a child who has had medical problems may have had this process disrupted. If he has been separated from you, poked, probed, and submitted to uncomfortable procedures, we would imagine the feelings of comfort and security that you attempted to instill would be somewhat unstable.

Because of all the factors that could prevent natural bonding from taking place, we at times offer to teach parents bonding techniques. We work to assist them in establishing a continuous bonding process.

We suggest that several times each day be set aside for parent and child to be comfortable and close with each other. During these times no toys, learning materials, or others distractions are introduced. It is simply a time for parent and child to get to know one another.

Activities we suggest for parents to do with a child during these times are those that are physically and mentally pleasurable and soothing. They include rocking, stroking, holding close, and singing or talking softly.

Parents who had been having difficulty and then began setting aside time for bonding to take place have reported that their feelings and their children's moods have changed considerably. Parents who at first were not totally comfortable handling their children became more comfortable and could therefore express their love and warmth more freely. Children who at first were resistive to the close physical contact began to sense that this parental handling was always very pleasant and comforting to them, and their responses become more trusting. Children whose attention was difficult to get at first would begin to look directly at a parent who was providing them with totally pleasant experiences.

If you feel that for any reason you have not firmly established a bond of trust and security with your child, we urge you to try some bonding techniques. Do not become discouraged if you do not sense immediate results, particularly with older children. Continue in your attempt. Try to imagine what may have prevented this process from taking place between the two of you and what may need to be undone before you can expect your child to feel totally secure. He did not know that any pain inflicted on him was only meant to help him, or that separation from you was at times necessary to save his life. He did not know that your insecurity in handling him was actually your fear of doing any harm to the fragile little person you loved. Give him and yourself plenty of time to overcome all of the unavoidable circumstances that prevented the continual bonding process. He will need to learn that the one thing he can always count on is your warmth, your closeness, and your love.

SUMMARY

In this section we have discussed factors that we feel contribute to the development of a positive self-image. To review briefly, they are 1) self-respect, 2) self-confidence, 3) a feeling of worthiness, 4) good body image, 5) pride, and 6) inner security. We have suggested ways that you can help your child develop these qualities.

While lists of suggestions appear simple enough on a printed page, we are well aware of the every day ups and downs that complicate your task. What we have attempted to do is increase your awareness. As life goes on, day to day, your child is indeed forming some self-image based on the reactions of you and others to him. His general mood and his behavior are indicators of whether or not he feels good about himself. If he is generally content, appears motivated, and responds to your love and attention, chances are good that you are doing things to instill a positive sense of self.

The idea of insuring the continuation of what you are doing at home to those outside of your home is another task. It is up to all of us who are involved with handicapped children to see that their handicaps and their strengths are appreciated and that the foundation is laid for them to proudly participate in the joys of living. As we teach our children, so must we teach others that our children are valuable and deserving individuals.

13. LOOKING AT THE FUTURE

We have encouraged you to take each day as it comes rather than worrying about the future. We know, however, that one cannot help but wonder what will happen to a child as he grows older. Parents of nonhandicapped as well as handicapped children have concerns about how their children will function as adults. Much of what parents do during a child's lifetime is in preparation for his adult living. Parents have shared with us that rather than spend a great deal of time worrying about the future of a handicapped child, it is wise to spend time preparing and paving the way for his life as an adult.

Most of the parents with whom we have worked have had to independently search out information bit by bit. The issue that seemed most difficult to deal with was deciding what would take place following graduation from the public school system. Parent's concerns centered around such questions as where he will live, if he will continue to go to school, whether he can get a job, and what kind of social life he will have.

In this chapter we will discuss the future as it applies to people with various handicapping conditions. We will share information and suggestions about adult education, employment, financial arrangements, living accommodations, needs for supervision and/or physical assistance, sexual roles, and long-term planning. It is our hope that by having a realistic picture of the options available to you, some of your concerns can be alleviated.

PHYSICALLY HANDICAPPED ADULTS

A student whose handicap affects only his motor performance is likely to graduate from the public school system with an academic background comparable to that of a nonhandicapped student.

Depending on his academic records and his career goals, college may or may not be a suitable choice. Other options for continuing education would include vocational, trade, or clerical schools.

Most high schools offer vocational counseling, which is an excellent way of becoming familiar with career opportunities. Such counseling gives a wide variety of choices from which someone can select a career for which he is best suited. Plans for continuing education or vocational training can then be based on career goals. In many schools, on-the-job training is included in such vocational counseling. In this way students can explore various jobs before selecting any particular employment.

When a physically handicapped person is seeking either college or job placement, it is necessary to determine what physical aids, adaptations, and assistance will be needed in order for him to function in a particular setting. By the time he leaves the public school system he hopefully will have been evaluated and provided with any aids he needs for mobility and/or communication—for example, crutches, walker, cane, braces, wheelchair, hand splints, typewriter, or communication board. Modern technology has provided us with sophisticated electronically controlled devices to aid the physically handicapped. The school system should be aware of any such devices that may benefit your child. You can also inquire about them through the largest rehabilitation hospital in your area. The veterans' hospitals also may be a good source for obtaining information about modern aids. This should be done, however, during your child's public school education so he is familiar and proficient with whatever aids he will use by the time he is ready to enter college or the work field.

The physical setting in which your child will need to function must also be considered. This would include the college or place of employment as well as the transportation coming and going from place to place. If your child will be wheelchair-bound, it will be necessary for any building he is in to have entrance and exit ramps, elevators if it is more than one story, doorways through which a wheelchair can fit, toileting facilities accessible from a wheelchair, and a work area at wheelchair height. If he is unable to use public transportation or drive an adapted vehicle, transportation arrangements will need to be made.

Another consideration for college or employment will be whether or not physical assistance is needed in any daily activities. If help is needed to get in and out of a wheelchair, carry books or lunch trays, remove clothing, or in any other routine activity, arrangements can be made with a willing fellow classmate or worker who will assist either voluntarily or for a small salary.

Living accommodations will likewise need to be evaluated for accessibility and the availability of physical assistance, if it is needed.

With regard to sexual performance, your physically handicapped child should be carefully evaluated at some time between puberty and his young adult life to determine how his or her sex life may or may not be affected. A neurologist should be able to make this determination. If your child is physiologically able to function sexually, but his handicapping condition interferes with his ability to perform physically, it is suggested that he seek sexual counseling to find methods and/or positions that will enable him to perform. Married couples should seek such counseling together. The person who is sexually active should have genetic studies done to determine whether or not his handicapping condition would in any way affect his offspring. Your physically handicapped child's sex education should otherwise be the same as that of a nonhandicapped person.

The child who is affected only physically by his handicapping condition can be taught from an early age to prepare for his future. Understanding his handicap and his physical limitations will help him to plan and build a future that utilizes his strengths and abilities. Self-understanding will also enable him to choose a life-style in which he can realistically function as a productive member of adult society.

VISUALLY IMPAIRED ADULTS

Like the physically handicapped person, the person whose only handicapping condition is visual impairment and who has been well prepared for independence as an adult has a variety of opportunities open to him.

The visually impaired child may or may not be mainstreamed in the public school system. In either case, with the exception of being provided with special learning aids and additional assistance (such as training for mobility, and for activities of daily living), his education should parallel that of a nonhandicapped child.

In seeking career counseling for the visually impaired person, the high school counselor may be of assistance. It would be wise, however, to seek further information about career opportunities from an agency that deals only with visually impaired adults, such as the American Council of the Blind. Oftentimes people unrealistically eliminate certain career choices which they believe require vision. If one is motivated toward a particular career where the need for vision is questionable, we encourage the individual to investigate thoroughly whether it would be possible to function in that career. The American Council of the Blind or a similar agency would be the best source of information if there is some question about the possibility of performing a particular job without vision.

Like the physically handicapped person, the visually impaired person should have been provided with any special aids that would enable independence during his public school education. If a braille typewriter has been provided by the school, it may be necessary for you to purchase one upon graduation. Your public library is a good source for books, tapes, and recording machines that are loaned to the visually impaired for educational or enjoyment purposes.

With regard to assistance that may be needed in a college or job placement, it is our experience that most visually impaired people function independently once they become familiar with a physical setting. An initial orientation period would be needed to familiarize oneself with the surroundings. If you have continued doubts as to how independently your child may be able to function, we urge you to speak to his teacher, counselor, or vocational trainer.

Transportation is likely to be a critical issue with respect to your child's independence. Public and private transportation arrangements should be made based upon your child's needs and where you live. Many visually impaired students are taught mobility and independent living skills from an early age. Become familiar with what skills your child has mastered and then determine what, if any, additional skills will be needed for total independent functioning.

Independent living arrangements are a feasible goal for many visually impaired citizens. Once again, the training your child has received throughout his school years (at home as well as in school) should stress such independence. For many, the opportunity to choose a desired life-style will be present. Such life-styles may include a career, marriage, and/or children.

It is helpful to direct your child from a young age to function as independently as possible. In doing so, your child will be better prepared to determine what life-style he desires and to select his career goals.

HEARING IMPAIRED ADULTS

The education of the hearing-impaired child is somewhat different from that of the physically handicapped or visually impaired child. The greatest disadvantage that may affect the quality of education he is able to receive is the communication barrier. The child who is hearing-impaired from birth will likely have speech and language problems. Although signing, lipreading, and/or oral skills are taught to the hearing-impaired child, this does not totally eliminate the barrier. Parents need to be aware that the hearing-impaired child who has a means of communication still lacks much of the quality of language. The hearing-impaired person who has been deaf since birth can be considered as having two handicapping conditions, one being the inability to hear and the other being the inability to communicate in the same manner as hearing people. Although highly intelligent, a person who is hearing-impaired from birth may exhibit learning difficulties, particularly in reading and writing courses where the primary emphasis is on language.

The hearing-impaired child may or may not be mainstreamed in the public school system. He is likely to be provided with special learning aids and assistance, although the academic material presented is much the same as that of a nonhandicapped child. Greater emphasis, however, is placed on areas in which language is critical.

Depending on the abilities and career goals, there is a variety of opportunities open to the hearing-impaired adult. As in the case of the physically handicapped and visually impaired, counseling would be advised both from the school and from an agency that deals only with hearing-impaired adults, such as the National Association of the Deaf, to determine whether college, vocational training, or on-the-job training would be the most suitable choice.

Adjustments and/or adaptations that may be needed in a college or job setting would be determined by the environment. For example, if the job requires primarily factory skills, a visual method of recognizing danger and safety alerts may be devised; if a job required communication with hearing people, a method of communicating or an interpreter may be required.

The modern advances in technology have brought us such inventions as captioned television, telecommunication devices for the deaf (tty-telephones for hearing-impaired and speech-impaired individuals), and alarm clocks and doorbells that work by light instead of sound. It is becoming increasingly common for interpreters to be available for important events such as medical appointments, spiritual meetings, political gatherings, or legal meetings. These advances have insured a truly independent life-style for many adults who are hearing-impaired. Those who have been well prepared for the future academically, physically, and socially should lead a productive and independent adult life.

EMOTIONALLY DISTURBED/BEHAVIORALLY DISORDERED ADULTS

The future possibilities of children who are diagnosed as having emotional disturbances or behavioral disorders cover a very wide range. It is difficult to prepare for your child's future since you cannot foresee what long-term effects behavior management techniques and therapy will have on altering his behavior. You can, however, set some guidelines for determining progress by recalling our discussion about the IEP (individualized educational plan). By reviewing yearly goals on the IEP, you can obtain some idea as to whether steady improvement is occurring. If goals continue to be mastered each year, it is possible that as your child continues in the public school system, he can be mainstreamed for more and more classes. Perhaps at some point he can be totally mainstreamed, needing only supplemental counseling services. If, however, you see goals remaining the same each year and no significant alterations in behavior are evident to you, it is possible your child will continue to need supervision.

In addition to behavior being in itself a determining factor, one must also consider how much behavior has affected the acquisition of academic skills. The future of the child who is academically productive in spite of inappropriate behavior will be somewhat different from the future of a child whose intelligence is masked by his behavior. A realistic view of your child's progress and the effect his handicapping condition has on productivity will help you to some degree in preparing for his future.

Vocational opportunities will likewise be dependent upon the progress your child demonstrates throughout his schooling. For some, it may be appropriate to explore career choices during the high school years. Others may find it more appropriate to spend this time investigating sheltered workshop arrangements or continued vocational training in programs developed to meet the needs of the special student. In thinking about your child's employment future, it would be wise to be as realistic as possible on a few counts. First, we must accept that only time will reveal the answers to many questions. It will be time that allows the measurement of the rate and extent of improvement in a child. Second, children who are diagnosed as having emotional or behavioral disorders exhibit a wide range of independent functioning. Some children may develop into totally independently functioning adults, while others will require maximum assistance.

The rate and extent of your child's improvement will not only affect his employment opportunities, but will also affect his ability to live independently. In the previous chapter we discussed alternatives to living within the family home. While some of these living arrangements required great degrees of independent functioning, others did not. The child who is unable to adjust on the one extreme may need total supervision or residential care. On the other extreme, the child who adjusts totally may go on to lead a "normal" adult life. Between these two extremes lie many possibilities. Some children may require continued counseling, but otherwise will be able to function independently. Others may need supervision periodically, but will be able to function independently with respect to many daily activities. Thus, some young adults would be able to live independently or in supervised living facilities, while others may require direct supervision from home or a residential facility.

It is very difficult to deal with uncertainties. The education of emotionally disturbed and behaviorally disordered children has changed significantly in recent years. The future for these children is more and more hopeful. We are encouraged by new techniques and increased interest in this area of special education. We believe parents should realistically face and be prepared for the decisions they may need to make regarding their children's futures. Our emphasis, however, would be on holding out hope and waiting until it is necessary to make definite plans regarding the future.

LEARNING DISABLED ADULTS

Only in recent years have learning disabilities been identified. Prior to that time children who are now recognized as having learning disabilities were frequently misdiagnosed as behavior problems, mentally handicapped, or underachievers. Now that learning disabilities are recognized and teaching methods are geared to meet particular needs, it is our guess that the future of learning disabled children will be much different from what it has been in past generations.

Still, much will depend on the severity of the learning disability. The child who can be structured and for whom an effective mode of learning has been found can likely be channeled to achieve his intellectual potential. Such a child may continue to have an area of weakness, but may compensate for it to the extent that it does not interfere with his overall ability to be successful in college, vocational training, or a career of his choice. The child who continues to have difficultly attending to a task and/or who cannot seem to use information he is receiving in a meaningful way will be more limited insofar as his future is concerned. It is our guess that such a child would need to be carefully channeled into a career or vocation where his training can be as carefully structured as was his educational experience.

For many adults who have learning disabilities, continued educational and vocational training go hand in hand. Such training is now offered at many local junior colleges or trade schools. In some states, colleges and universities have also devised special curricula to challenge each student's strengths while minimizing his disabilities.

Independent living, for many learning disabled adults, is likely to be a realistic goal. This goal, however, is highly dependent upon whether or not the young adult can find and maintain gainful employment. For this reason we encourage you to investigate various types of training facilities and opportunities before your child graduates from high school.

There is, however, one further point we would like to make about children with learning disabilities. Because their differences are more subtle than those of children who have obvious handicaps, peers may not recognize their problems. They may have difficulty with socialization. The self-image you have helped to build and the social skills you have taught will be of great importance as your child grows toward maturity. The future of a child with learning disabilities will depend to a great extent on whether his weaknesses or his strengths have been emphasized and reinforced in his childhood.

MENTALLY HANDICAPPED ADULTS

Preparation for the future of a mentally handicapped child will depend on his specific diagnosis. The education provided for mentally handicapped students is geared to prepare educable (EMH) and trainable (TMH) children with skills that are marketable when they leave the public school system at age twenty-one. Emphasis will be on vocational training and will hopefully be sufficient to make these children partially or totally self-supporting adults. As much academic material as these children can handle is included in their educational programming. In academics, however, the emphasis is on those subjects that will help them improve their job skills, That is, reading and math are emphasized over geography and music.

There is a range of possibilities for employment of mentally handicapped adults. The ultimate opportunity would be that of competitive employment. By this we mean employment in the open job market. Educable and trainable adults can possibly function well in jobs that are available on the open market and should be encouraged to compete for jobs for which they are qualified. Some people need on-the-job supervision, in which case a sheltered workshop would be the most appropriate employment setting. Your school vocational counselor should be well acquainted with your child's abilities and job skills, and should be prepared to direct you in the proper course of action prior to your child's graduation from public school.

The preparation for the future of children who are diagnosed as severe and profoundly mentally handicapped would involve the teaching of self-help skills and activities of daily living. Emphasis would be on teaching dressing, feeding, toileting, and simple household tasks, to give the child as much independence as possible as an adult.

Living arrangements for mentally handicapped citizens would depend to a great extent on their ability to be self-supporting as well as self-sufficient. Community or independent living would necessitate being able to handle one's own finances; make purchases independently; take care of meals, laundry, and household chores; and travel independently in the community. There are mentally handicapped people who are capable of community living, and it is a realistic option for those who show the ability to function on their own.

To find out if there is a community residential facility in your area, you can contact your local mental health association. It should be mentioned that in some areas families of mentally handicapped children and adult citizens have worked cooperatively to establish such a facility within a community. Some raise private funds to do so, while others seek government assistance. Your local mental health association can also guide you on how to implement a plan for a facility if you are interested in such an undertaking.

For adults who are not candidates for independent or moderately supervised community living, there appear to be only two options available upon graduation from school: 1) remaining at home under direct parental care, and 2) residential placement in a facility where their special needs can be met and family members can visit and be actively involved in their lives.

Decisions regarding living arrangements need to be carefully thought out based on your child's needs, your family's needs, and financial considerations. If it is an arrangement away from home, a trial period may be needed for all those involved to make adjustments and determine whether or not the proper decision has been made. As we have previously stated, no decision regarding living arrangements need be final or unalterable.

The sex education of mentally handicapped children is extremely important. We must acknowledge that most are physiologically the same as nonhandicapped people, and therefore have the same sexual urges. The special need they exhibit is the need to channel their physiological urges into appropriate sexual behavior. These children, like any children, should be taught as much as they are able to comprehend about sexual differences and functions. They should be helped to understand their own bodies and feelings insofar as possible. In addition and probably most important, many of them need to be taught when and where it is permissable to engage in sexual activity. That is, they must learn that privacy is essential. They need to respect their own privacy and the privacy of others. If a child is unable to make judgments regarding this, parental discipline may be needed to discourage inappropriate sexual behaviors. This does not necessarily mean that sexual activity should be discouraged altogether, but that the child should be taught in what place and at what times it is permissible.

If dating or marriage is a consideration, there is a definite need for sexual counseling. Parents along with young adults should seek such counseling from the school or from a mental health association so that sound decisions can be reached regarding genetic counseling, parenting responsibilities, birth control, and other issues.

Throughout our writing we have used the terms *appropriate* and *inappropriate* with regard to behavior. We feel these terms are particularly important to the future of mentally handicapped children. With significant progress in the education of these children in recent years, many opportunities are available to them that were not available in the past. These children are no longer lumped into a single category of uneducables and isolated from society to lead hopeless and fruitless lives. Each of them is individually assessed and educated according to his abilities. We often find that although children with mental handicaps possess certain abilities, they lack the judgment, discipline, and social skills that will enable them to function well in the adult community. If fact, those who have good job skills but poor self-discipline and socialization skills are less likely to be successful in employment than those who are socially appropriate and well disciplined but have lesser job skills. We must assume that some of these children cannot interpret moral values and social standards of behavior. They simply need to be taught through firm but loving parental discipline what is and is not acceptable behavior. Their future happiness and independence may well depend on how strictly you have enforced a standard of behavior in your home.

Parents can be fairly well prepared for the future of a mentally handicapped or developmentally delayed child. Based on what has taken place during the school years, we can develop a realistic picture of a child's future potential. With guidance and counseling from the school and perhaps other agencies, choices can be made from the options we have discussed regarding employment and living arrangements.

Based on the recent progress in the areas of education and neurology, we continue to hope for still more insight into the process of mental development. With each new milestone that is reached, mentally handicapped people become less limited in their capacity to live happy and productive lives.

MULTIPLE HANDICAPPED ADULTS

In preparing for the future of the multiple handicapped child it will be necessary to 1) identify the primary handicapping condition, 2) identify all the handicapping conditions, 3) identify the level at which the individual is able to function given those conditions.

It is important to identify the primary condition because it is this condition that will likely remain the overriding concern in education as well as vocational training. For example, if the child's primary handicap is mental impairments, educational skills during the school years would have a different emphasis than if the child's primary difficulties were in the area of motor skills.

Identifying all your child's handicapping conditions will allow you to plan more completely for his future. It is also critical because so many problems are interdependent. For example, an individual who has severely handicapped upper extremities (hands and arms) and also has a hearing impairment would not be able to communicate by relying on a single system. An alternative means of communication would be required. Identifying the primary handicapping conditions and determining how the secondary conditions affect overall performance will provide you with a realistic view of your child's abilities.

Anticipating the future of children with multiple handicaps is like anticipating anyone's future—it is largely dependent upon the individual's level of independence. An example of this would be if a child was ambulatory and also possessed good independent living skills. It is likely that residential and/or community placement could be found. It is also likely that this individual would be able to find work in a sheltered shop or within the community. On the other hand, if an individual was nonambulatory, could not perform any of the activities necessary for independent living (toileting, feeding, and so forth), it would be very difficult to find appropriate residential and/ or community living arrangements. It is likely that it would also be difficult to locate adequate employment in either a sheltered workshop or job within the community.

As a parent, it will be necessary for you to identify how well your child functions with the multiple handicaps he demonstrates. This is usually not possible to do early in life. By identifying levels of independence, his primary handicapping conditions, and his ability to function with those conditions, you will then be able to look to the options discussed previously.

GENERAL DISCUSSION

As is true of your child's public school education, his adult experience should also parallel that of a nonhandicapped person insofar as possible. With this in mind, we go back to the basic statement we make repeatedly: Recognize your child's actual needs and make provisions for them to be met either by you or by others that you and your child trust. Recognize your child's strengths and abilities and make certain they are developed to their fullest potential. In other words, see your child as a total person—how his handicapping condition limits his function and how he functions apart from his handicapping condition. If you have a realistic view of your child by the time he reaches young adulthood, you should be well prepared to help him make good decisions about his future.

In thinking about all the aspects of daily living, there is a great deal more to consider than education, employment, and living arrangements. We will discuss several topics in general. Some have already been mentioned under the individual handicapping condition, but need additional clarification.

Many handicapped adults are able to handle their finances independently. Those who are totally self-supporting fit this category. Some need minimal or moderate assistance, and in some cases it may be necessary for family members to take total charge of financial matters. In the case of an emotionally disturbed or mentally handicapped child it would be particularly important to carefully assess your child's ability to at least share in the decision-making process regarding money matters. Many of these children know how to bank their earnings and have checking accounts in their own names. It is important that they be given as much responsibility as they are able to handle in financial matters. Financial independence, partial or total, seems to be a primary goal for all young adults. The recognition that your child can assume responsibility for this area of his life is an indication to him that you view him as an adult.

We have discussed sexuality as it pertains to physically and mentally handicapped adults. The extreme variations that exist between emotionally disturbed adults would make it difficult to make general suggestions that pertain to them. Some may function sexually like nonhandicapped people. Others may exhibit inappropriate sexual behaviors, in which case it would be necessary to attempt to alter such behaviors. The same behavior management techniques that have been employed to alter other behaviors would apply as well in the alteration of inappropriate sexual behavior. It is our opinion that all adults with a handicapping condition who will possibly be sexually active should receive counseling regarding parenting responsibilities, genetic factors, communicable diseases, birth control, and so forth.

We have discussed socialization as a subject by itself. It bears repeating when we look at the future of handicapped citizens. There exists a great danger of isolation when the formal educational process ends. School inherently provides much of the social environment for handicapped children. If your child continues his schooling, works in a job setting where he can mingle with his peers, or moves into a residential setting, he will continue to have opportunities for socialization. If, however, your child spends the majority of his time at home or on a job where he is isolated from others, opportunities for socialization in his adult life will need to be created.

The child who has been mainstreamed in school will no doubt adjust easily in the mainstream of adult society. Those, however, who have been in special education classes throughout their school years may feel most comfortable maintaining the friendships they have established with other handicapped people. Parents often arrange for socialization with old friends to continue after graduation from school. While their children still attend school they form parent groups and exchange addresses and phone numbers so that they can remain in contact following graduation. We have already discussed, in the section on socialization, some of the possibilities for activities in which young adult groups can participate, as well as other ways aside from school contact to form groups.

When we speak of long-term planning, we refer to what will happen to your child in the event of your death or when you are no longer able to care for him yourself. If you do not foresee the possibility of his becoming a totally self-supporting, self-sufficient adult, it is important to plan for him when he will no longer have the benefit of your help. These plans may be in the form of wills, trusts, Social Security benefits, or public assistance. Review our chapter on financial concerns and determine the best arrangement (or combination of arrangements) for you and your child.

CONCLUSION

When we speak of looking at the future, we are dealing in an area of great uncertainty. This is true of the future of any child, handicapped or nonhandicapped. What we are doing is making guesses based on the present and the past. Our guesses take into consideration the quality and characteristics of a child as well as the quality and characteristics of the society in which he lives.

There are many issues which continue to have a negative effect on the future of handicapped citizens. Some of these issues pertain to financial considerations; others are centered around discrimination against the handicapped citizen. Discrimination has been evidenced in employment, housing, and other areas of civil rights.

For example, in the area of employment, handicapped citizens may not be hired for jobs due to physical appearance; they may be the first to be laid off or fired; they may not be paid the minimum wage. Architectural barriers may prevent access to various job opportunities.

Some community groups have attempted to exclude and discriminate against handicapped citizens by preventing group homes and supervised living facilities from being developed in residential areas. Some have successfully prevented them from renting and buying homes in certain areas. They too have used architectural barriers to prohibit handicapped citizens from certain opportunities within the community.

Voting rights, driving privileges, and the need for advocates (individuals who protect the rights of handicapped citizens who are unable to represent themselves) have all been recently debated. In looking at the future of handicapped citizens, it is necessary that we continuously look to eliminate such discrimination and develop not only community awareness but also community acceptance.

Advances in medicine, technology, and education have altered the quality of life for all people. Legislation and social awareness have created a new morality. People have established different value systems based on a changing economy. In light of a changing society, it would be aimless to agonize over the question, "What will happen to my child as an adult?" The question we must address is, "How can I prepare my child for adulthood?" There is a big difference between passively waiting to see how one will be affected by society and actively preparing to live in society as an adult.

Based on the present and the past, we can only see positive social, educational, medical, technical, legislative, and economic change with regard to the future of handicapped citizens. If you and your child are well prepared, he will reap the benefit of all positive change. If you and he are not prepared, positive change will not affect his life.

We have basically discussed two general areas of preparation: 1) practical or economic preparation, which would include his education/vocational training, determining his means of support, making living arrangements, and long-term financial planning, and 2) social preparation, which would include the teaching of social skills, providing opportunities for establishing relationships, and establishing guidelines for future social-emotional outlets.

Generally, what we have said in discussing each of the various handicaps is, identify your child's abilities and limitations. Look then at society and identify the abilities and limitations of the system into which your child will be integrated. You will find that in some ways your child will easily fit into the system. In other ways society is limited in its ability to integrate handicapped citizens.

Your preparation will involve utilizing every available advantage. The advantages include all of your child's abilities and every legal, social, and financial provision that the system makes for a child such as yours. In other words, if your child learns to give everything he has and take advantage of all the rights and opportunities society has to offer him, he will have the best possible future.

As parents, your involvement in the transition to an adult world will be crucial. Those children whose handicaps are less limited will need your guidance to minimize the effects of their handicapping condition and make the maturation process a smooth and natural event. Those who are more severely handicapped will need you as their advocate to assure that the system meets all the financial and moral obligations due them as adults.

As you reach the point in your lives when your child will be leaving the school system, you will no doubt experience some feelings of insecurity. Knowing your alternatives for the future and seeing school graduation as a natural milestone may alleviate some of your fears. For some it will mean finding a job, for some a supervised work experience, and for some moving away from home to a college or residential care setting. Any of these possibilities represent natural change at an appropriate age. The loss of school as a sanctuary and the entrance into an adult world where one must face new challenges is part of the maturation process. Even the most severely handicapped are not exempt from experiencing this stage of personal growth.

Whether the challenge your child faces as an adult involves becoming a great physicist, learning to assemble nuts and bolts, or learning to relate to a new person with a smile or hug, it is up to you to have confidence in his ability to deal with challenges on his own. Have faith in the parenting job you are doing and faith in a system that continues to make positive change with regard to its handicapped citizens.

We build for and envision the future of our handicapped children. In building for the future we acknowledge their special needs and recognize that society provides some answers for their special care. We deal with realities as they exist today. In envisioning the future we look to medicine to find cures. We look to society for the key that will enable total integration. We look with hope and promise to tomorrow.

P.S. . . . . .

The families we work with have given us insights which enable us to work with a better understanding of the issues involved in parenting the handicapped child. Your experience has given you insights that are likely to inspire others to grow, develop, and accept individuals who are handicapped. There are things you can do as an individual, or as part of a group that would serve to increase awareness and educate people to the critical issues which surround handicapping conditions. In this final section we would like to offer ideas and suggestions about what you can do for others.

If you cannot or do not desire to be part of a group effort, there is much you can do as an individual that can have a positive effect on the lives of handicapped people. Your primary roles as an individual would be to make your opinion known and increase awareness. Examples of how you might do so are by responding to the media, communicating with your legislators and gaining the support of your local library as a center for distributing current information.

Media (television, newspapers, etc.) today reach a vast audience and affect the opinions of many people. It is unfortunate that some continue to use them in an irresponsible manner. Poor television programs which inaccurately depict handicapping conditions continue to be shown. Misleading articles in newspapers, books, and magazine are still being printed. Such blatant misrepresentation continues to foster misconceptions and does nothing to end discrimination against handicapped people.

As an individual you have the opportunity to protest or applaud media coverage. Write to the network stations and let them know your thoughts on specific programs. Do not forget to also write letters to sponsors of such programs. Letters to editors of magazines and journals would also be an effective means of protesting or supporting specific articles. Do not worry about typing, grammar, etc. If there is a point to be made—make it!

Legislation continues to be a powerful tool in improving the quality of life for all handicapped persons. As an individual it is possible for you to be effective by finding out who your representatives are and writing letters about your feelings. Too often people convince themselves that a single letter would not make a difference.

If a letter is directed to your representative or a special interest group, it certainly can make a difference.

As an individual you may also make effective changes in your local library. Most libraries actively solicit recommendations and requests from their patrons. Such requests need not be for new books only, but may include magazine and journal subscriptions, cassettes and records. Your librarian should be able to better direct your requests to the proper people.

Individuals *can* effect changes.

If you have the need or interest and feel that you may profit from joining a parent or professional support group, there may be one which already exists in your community. Many national groups have smaller chapters located throughout the nation. For example, United Cerebral Palsy (UCP) is a national organization. Throughout the states it has many local chapters which meet monthly or bimonthly. There are many such support groups which exist on a national and/or local level.

Existing support groups engage in such activities as providing speakers, working toward changes in legislation, fund raising, providing general support, and offering social experiences to parents and families.

These groups create a natural setting where families can be working toward common goals while gaining support from each other.

Other groups which you may join are those that may or may not be specific to parents of handicapped children. A parent-teacher organization is an example of such a group. These groups exist in educational, workshop, and residential settings. Whether your group consists totally of parents with children who have special needs or not, you can use this forum to better develop awareness and provide education for other parents and educators.

An example of how these parent-teacher organizations are promoting understanding between handicapped and nonhandi-capped people is that some district schools and special schools are teaming up and forming "sister schools" relationships. Children from both schools send letters, pictures, or notes to inform each other of some of their activities. Gradually the children are introduced through school functions, field trips, etc. It is an excellent example of children becoming aware and educated about differences in people from an early age.

Membership in a fraternal organization (Lions, Elks, Shriners, etc.) often provides an opportunity to help in yet another way. Many such groups raise funds to provide equipment and medical care to those in need. These groups have made a major contribution to the cause of improving the quality of life for handicapped people.

For people who live in areas where support groups have not been established, or those that desire different kinds of support than established groups offer, developing your own support group may be an alternative to consider. Developing a local support group may be easier than you think.

You can gather names or create a list of potential members from the program your child is presently in. Schools, workshops, residential facilities, hospitals, and similar places all provide a starting place.

Your group can serve many purposes ranging from providing special educational experiences to simply being a social gathering.

Groups which provide educational and informational material do so in a number of ways. They hire speakers to discuss specific disabilities, aspects of parenting, or Issues pertaining to family life. Speakers may be doctors, educators, legislators, or representitives of special interest groups. Parent groups which consist primarily of young or new parents often invite parents of older children with similar handicaps to speak at their meetings.

Another way to increase members' knowledge is by developing a newsletter or bulletin. Group members may include their recommendations of articles, books, and speakers. They may use the newsletter to share new ideas, experiences, or simply to offer comfort and support.

Parent groups have also sponsored trips for their members. Such trips may include visits to residential settings, vocational workshops, public and private schools, etc. By visiting as a group, parents feel more at ease asking questions or discussing advantages and disadvantages of certain programs. They typically express the comfort they feel by going through such new and sometimes stressful experiences with others who understand their feelings.

Parent groups also act as fund-raising committees. Some have used fund raisers for the specific medical or therapeutic needs of an individual. Other groups use the money toward purchasing equipment or making group field trips. Groups which have an interest in a specific disability may use monies to support a legislator, lobby group, or contribute to research foundations. Needless to say, fund raising will always be an important part of parent groups.

A valuable service which has been provided by parent support groups is that of helping new parents of handicapped children through the initial adjustment period. One aspect of that service is to visit maternity wards where there is a parent of a newly diagnosed infant. Another would be a visit to parents of a newly diagnosed child upon the referral of a doctor or hospital. It is very comforting to a parent during this time to have the friendship and empathy of one who has already "been down the road."

The formation of sibling groups has been deemed a very important activity by some parents. In such groups, sisters and brothers of handicapped children meet to share common interests and concerns. For younger siblings these groups often begin as play sessions and develop into friendship and support groups as the children mature. Older children can use the group environment to openly express and explore their feelings with those they feel will understand.

Many parent groups—whether they are part of a national organization or only a local group—have taken up the cause of improving community relations. As parents and educators we tend to assume a certain degree of recognition and acceptance of handicapped citizens on the part of society. In many cases this assumption is erroneous.

The general public is not always as aware of the issues and facts regarding handicapped citizens as we would like them to be.

The first goal of parent groups, who are working to improve community relations, is to foster community awareness. By using newsletters, newspapers, and local media, parent groups have increased awareness of the fact that handicapped citizens do exist in the community.

Many parents have found strong and consistent support from community groups such as local school and hospital boards, local political groups, fraternal groups and clergy. These community leaders are in a position to recognize and facilitate positive changes at a local level.

Once a sense of awareness has been created, groups can then begin to work on community education. With awareness comes recognition; with education comes acceptance.

Educating the community consists of providing accurate and current information about handicapped citizens. It provides the community with a way to explore pertinent issues such as housing, employment, and education. Successful education of the community will be achieved when the community as a whole recognizes and accepts its handicapped citizens and refuses to tolerate segregation and discrimination.

Parent groups then act as a means of providing opportunities for parents to grow educationally, socially, and emotionally. They also serve to help a community to recognize and accept its handicapped citizens.

In this closing section we have discussed several ways that you can become actively involved in improving the quality of life for other handicapped people and their families. The progress that is made will depend on our individual and group efforts. If we touch one life, we have achieved success. If we change one opinion or dispel one myth we have achieved a victory. If, together, we can change the course of events for the future toward the goal of mutual understanding, we have triumphed.

We repeat, "We look with hope and promise to tomorrow." Each of us and all of us can be instrumental in making the promise we have become fulfilled and the hopes we have become realities.

INDEX